MW00399037

Jewish Life in Mr. Lincoln's City

Jewish Historical Society of Greater Washington

Lillian and Albert Small Jewish Museum

Edited by Laura Cohen Apelbaum and Claire Uziel

Publication of this book was made possible
by generous contributions from:

Albert H. Small

Robert H. Smith

Doris and Robert I. Silverman Endowment
Herman-Silverman Family Endowment
in support of Jewish Historical Society publications
and educational programming

Laura and Perry Apelbaum and Faye Cohen

For 50 years, the Jewish Historical Society of Greater Washington and its Lillian and Albert Small Jewish Museum have been chronicling the story of the Jewish community in Washington, D.C., and the suburbs of Maryland and Northern Virginia.

In 1969, the Society galvanized the community to preserve the historic 1876 Adas Israel Synagogue, the oldest in the Washington area. After extensive renovation and restoration, the synagogue was rededicated and opened to the public as the Lillian and Albert Small Jewish Museum.

The Society maintains the only community-wide archive of the local Jewish community. The collections include personal papers, oral histories, organizational records, and more than 1,500 photographs that trace the history of the Jewish community from its mid-19th century origins to the present day. Public programming includes walking tours, lectures, and book talks. More than 1,000 schoolchildren participate each year in educational field trips and enjoy living history performances.

The Society also publishes *The Record*, a journal of local Jewish history. For more than twenty years, the Jewish Historical Society has mounted exhibits based on original research that have traveled throughout the metropolitan community. The Society is a local leader in the concept of "public space Judaism," mounting exhibits and programs in venues that are accessible and welcoming to the greater public.

Jewish Historical Society of Greater Washington
Lillian and Albert Small Jewish Museum
701 Fourth Street, NW
Washington, D.C. 20001
(202) 789-0900 info@jhsgw.org www.jhsgw.org

Editors: Laura Cohen Apelbaum and Claire Uziel
First edition
Designed by Jeanne Krohn | Krohn Design
Printed by HBP, Inc., Hagerstown, Maryland

Cover image and pages 21, 83, 111, 152: Barry Rice enlisted in the Union Army in Colorado. After the Civil War, his sister Hannah married Bernard Nordlinger, a former Confederate bugler who opened a shoe store in Georgetown. Photo courtesy of Robin Nordlinger Leiman

ISBN 978-0-615-27879-7
Library of Congress Control Number 2009922914

Table of Contents

Foreword 1
Laura Cohen Apelbaum

About the Contributors 5

A Civil War Timeline 8

Introduction 11
Dr. Jonathan Sarna

Jewish Life in Mr. Lincoln's City 21
Text and images from the exhibition

Lincoln and the Jews 57
Harold Holzer

Virginian Jews in the Civil War 71
Dr. Melvin I. Urofsky

"Giving our all to the poor soldiers:"
Jewish Women in the Civil War 85
Dr. Pamela S. Nadell

Ulysses S. Grant and the Jews:
An Unsolved Mystery 99
Dr. John Y. Simon

The Jewish Community of Washington, D.C.,
During the Civil War 113
Robert Shosteck

List of Jewish Residents of Washington, D.C.,
and Alexandria, Virginia 154

Index 164

Foreword

Civil War history is tangible in our city. Its tales are well known and connected to many local landmarks: the White House, Ford's Theater, Fort Stevens, the Lincoln Cottage, and the Willard Hotel, among others. The story of Jewish life in our city and across the river in Alexandria, however, never has been fully told.

This book, based on an exhibition of the same title, was created as part of the celebration of the 200th anniversary of the birth of President Abraham Lincoln. It introduces Jewish residents of both Washington and Alexandria who lived their lives during the tumultuous four years of the Civil War.

The idea of more fully exploring Jewish life during the Civil War was inspired by Dr. Gary Zola, Executive Director of the American Jewish Archives in Cincinnati. While visiting our exhibition, *Jewish Washington*, on display at the National Building Museum in 2005, Dr. Zola spoke of the upcoming bicentennial of Lincoln's birth. Several stories in that exhibit hinted at the Jewish role in the Civil War, including tales of Jewish immigrant soldiers on both sides of the conflict, the early days of Washington Hebrew and Beth El Hebrew congregations, and the Lansburgh brothers, owners of the famed department store, who were the first contributors to the city's first Lincoln statue.

Though more than 10,000 books have been published about Abraham Lincoln, this one adds a unique perspective. It contains the complete exhibition text accompanied by historic images, most from our archival collections. In addition we are pleased that our contributors permitted us to publish articles that give a fuller view of Jewish life in the area and within the context of American life at the time. Dr. Jonathan Sarna graciously provides an introduction to the history of Jewish life during the Civil War; Dr. Pam Nadell reveals the ways in which women's lives were affected and how they participated in the war effort, North and South. Stories of Jewish life in Alexandria and other Virginia communities are provided by Dr. Mel Urofsky. Harold Holzer focuses on President Lincoln's relationship with the Jewish community, including anecdotes about Lincoln's Jewish friends.

We are indebted to each of our contributors for their advice, stimulating articles, and support of this volume. Their friendship and historical insight has enriched our work.

Robert Shosteck, of blessed memory, a past president of the Jewish Historical Society of Greater Washington, wrote an article in 1967 about Jewish life in Washington during the Civil War that has become a primary text for researchers and historians of the era. We are delighted to reprint an edited version of that article.

We thank the family of Dr. John Y. Simon for permitting us to republish an article John wrote for us in 1995. Dr. Simon was the leading authority on Ulysses S. Grant and the editor of the U.S. Grant papers. His wit and wisdom enable us to understand a difficult chapter in American Jewish history — Grant's issuance of Orders No. 11 — expelling "the Jews as a class" from areas under his authority in the West. John passed away in June 2008, and we still feel the sorrow of his loss.

We appreciate the help of editors David Bruce Smith, Barbara Shapiro, and Dr. Sherry Levy-Reiner, who helped shape this book's content. As usual, designer Jeanne Krohn translated an idea into a reality. David McKenzie and Wendy Turman patiently read drafts, checked credits, and made sure all our details were correct. Joel Wind, as ever, provided help whenever needed. A special thanks to Claire Uziel, my co-editor and partner in overseeing production of the book.

Finally, without the support of many others, this book would not be in your hands. The donors to the exhibition are listed on page 153 of this volume. Robert H. Smith's generous gift toward this book initiated its publication. Proceeds from the Doris and Robert I. Silverman Endowment and the Herman-Silverman Family Foundation Endowment were critical to moving the project forward. My mother, Faye Cohen, also provided support.

A capstone contribution from Albert H. Small ensured this volume's publication and helped us realize the vision of a work that would enhance and expand on the exhibition.

I was privileged to grow up in a household that valued history. The Civil War was a topic at our dinner table sparking my interest. Fuel was thrown on that spark by family friend Ralph G. Newman, proprietor of the famed Abraham Lincoln Bookstore in Chicago. My parents' insistence that we travel with Mr. Newman to battlefields on Civil War Roundtable trips instilled in me a love of history in authentic places and a desire to pursue history as a vocation. Mr. Newman's ability to make history literally come to life inspires me to dedicate this book to his memory.

Laura Cohen Apelbaum, Executive Director
Jewish Historical Society of Greater Washington

About the Contributors

Harold Holzer is one of the country's leading authorities on Abraham Lincoln and the political culture of the Civil War era. A prolific author and lecturer, he serves as co-chairman of the Abraham Lincoln Bicentennial Commission. His new book, *Lincoln President-Elect*, is the thirty-first he has authored, coauthored, or edited on the subject of our sixteenth president. For his scholarship on the Civil War and President Lincoln, he received a 2008 National Humanities Medal from the National Endowment for the Humanities. He is Senior Vice President for External Affairs at The Metropolitan Museum of Art in New York.

A version of Holzer's article appeared in Lincoln and the Jews: The Last Best Hope of Earth *(The Skirball Cultural Center, 2002) and is reprinted here with the author's permission.*

Dr. Pamela S. Nadell is the Inaugural Patrick Clendenen Professor of History and Director of the Jewish Studies Program at American University. She is the author of *Women Who Would Be Rabbis: A History of Women's Ordination, 1889-1985* (1998) and *Conservative Judaism in America* (1988), and editor of *American Jewish Women's History: A Reader* (2003) and *Women and American Judaism: Historical Perspectives* (co-edited with Jonathan D. Sarna, 2001). Past chair of the Academic Council of the American Jewish Historical Society, she now chairs the Academic Advisory Council of the Jewish Historical Society of Greater Washington.

Dr. Jonathan Sarna is the Joseph H. & Belle R. Braun Professor of American Jewish History at Brandeis University and Director of its Hornstein Jewish Professional Leadership Program. Named by *The Forward* as one of America's fifty most influential American Jews, he is a leading commentator on American Jewish history, religion, and life. Dr. Sarna has written, edited, or co-edited more than twenty books, including the acclaimed *American Judaism: A History* (recipient of 2004 National Jewish Book Award from the Jewish Book Council) and his newly released *A Time to Every Purpose: Letters to a Young Jew.*

Dr. Sarna's introduction is condensed and adapted from his book, American Judaism: A History *(New Haven: Yale University Press, 2004), 112-124, where full documentation may be found. Reprinted with permission.*

Robert Shosteck was a founder and the first president of the Jewish Historical Society of Greater Washington. He was also a founder, editor, and frequent contributor to the Society's journal, *The Record.* After working for B'nai B'rith International as director of research in its Vocational Service Bureau for 26 years, he became curator of the B'nai B'rith Klutznick Exhibit Halls until his retirement in 1975. He died in 1979.

Shosteck's article is an edited version of "The Jewish Community of Washington, D.C., during the Civil War," American Jewish Historical Quarterly *56 (March 1967), 319-347, and is reprinted with permission of the American Jewish Historical Society.*

Dr. John Y. Simon was an award-winning historian who spent more than four decades teaching at Southern Illinois University. Leader of the Ulysses S. Grant Association, Simon edited the acclaimed 31-volume *Papers of Ulysses S. Grant.* Simon, also an authority on the Civil War and Abraham Lincoln, won the Lincoln Prize for outstanding scholarship about the late president, a lifetime achievement award from The Lincoln Forum, and an Award of Merit from the Illinois State Historical Society, among other accolades. He died in 2008.

Simon's article originally appeared in The Record, *21 (Jewish Historical Society of Greater Washington, 1995) 24-33, and is reprinted with permission from his family.*

Dr. Melvin I. Urofsky is Professor of Law & Public Policy and Professor Emeritus of History at Virginia Commonwealth University. He writes widely on constitutional history and current policy issues and has been the editor of *The Journal of Supreme Court History* for 15 years. Co-editor of seven volumes of Brandeis letters, he also has written numerous books including *The Levy Family and Monticello, 1842-1923: Saving Thomas Jefferson's House*, and *Commonwealth and Community: The Jewish Experience in Virginia.* His recent biography of Justice Louis D. Brandeis was published by Pantheon in September 2009.

Urofsky's article is adapted from Commonwealth and Community: The Jewish Experience in Virginia *(Virginia Historical Society and Jewish Community Federation of Richmond, 1997), and is reprinted with the author's permission.*

A Civil War Timeline

1860

November 6
Abraham Lincoln elected 16th president

December 20
South Carolina secedes

1861

February 9
Seven seceded states (SC, MS, FL, AL, GA, LA, TX) form the Confederate States of America

March 4
President Abraham Lincoln's first inauguration

March 24
Union forces occupy Alexandria, Virginia

April 12
Civil War starts at Fort Sumter, South Carolina

July 21
Confederates win First Battle of Bull Run near Manassas, Virginia

August 24
Southerner Eugenia Phillips arrested for spying in Washington

1862

April 16
District of Columbia Emancipation Act frees about 3,000 slaves

July 17
President Lincoln signs law authorizing rabbis to serve as battlefield chaplains

August 28-30
Second Battle of Bull Run near Manassas, Virginia, won by Confederates

December 4
Bernhard Behrend asks President Lincoln to grant Jewish soldiers leave for Sabbath

December 17
Major General Ulysses S. Grant issues General Orders No. 11, expelling Jews from the Department of the Tennessee (including parts of southern Illinois, Kentucky, and Mississippi)

1863

January 1
President Lincoln issues Emancipation Proclamation, freeing slaves in the Southern states

Background: View of Washington in 1861.
Courtesy of Library of Congress

January 17
Jewish emissaries persuade President Lincoln to revoke General Orders No. 11

July 1-3
Battle of Gettysburg, Pennsylvania, turns the tide in the war

July 31
Washington Hebrew Congregation dedicates first building, at 8th and I Streets, NW

1864

Alexandria's Beth El Hebrew Congregation hires first spiritual leader

March 10
Lincoln promotes Ulysses S. Grant to command all Union armies

May 5-7
Battle of the Wilderness, Virginia. Leopold Karpeles later awarded the Medal of Honor for bravery

July 11-12
Lincoln witnesses Battle of Fort Stevens within the District's boundaries

1865

March 4
President Lincoln's second inauguration

April 9
General Robert E. Lee surrenders to Grant at Appomattox, Virginia

April 14
John Wilkes Booth mortally wounds President Lincoln in Ford's Theatre; Dr. Charles Liebermann is among those called to his bedside

April 15
President Lincoln dies

April 19
Lincoln's funeral procession includes 125 marchers from Washington Hebrew Congregation; Beth El Hebrew holds a memorial service for President Lincoln

December 6
Slavery abolished with ratification of 13th Amendment

1868

April 15
Unveiling of one of the country's first memorial statues of Lincoln. Lansburgh brothers among the donors. Statue still stands at 4th and D Streets, NW

INTRODUCTION

Dr. Jonathan D. Sarna

The Civil War that divided the Washington community and the nation as a whole divided American Jewry as well. The bulk of America's 150,000 Jews, most of them new immigrants, lived in the North and supported the Union. The rest, something over 25,000 Jews, lived in the South and supported the Confederacy. Some on both sides, including the foremost Jewish religious leaders of the day, Isaac Leeser and Isaac Mayer Wise, would have compromised over slavery or acquiesced to secession rather than go to war in defense of principle. They sought to promote peace.

Jews, as this book demonstrates, fought on both sides of the Civil War. Some eight to ten thousand Jews, mostly recent immigrants, donned uniforms, and at least fifty rose through the ranks to become officers. Religion generally posed no barrier to military promotion. Indeed, one Union officer actually won his position *because* he was a Jew. Observing that "we have not yet appointed a Hebrew," Abraham Lincoln in 1862, ordered the Secretary of War to assign C. M. Levy, the son-in-law of Rabbi Morris Raphall of New York, to the post of Assistant Quarter-Master, with the rank of Captain.

w of Abraham Lincoln's first
ıguration, March 4, 1861,
ıe United States Capitol.

In the Confederacy, of course, one of the most brilliant and accomplished Jews of the 19th century, Judah P. Benjamin, reached the pinnacle of power. He served at different times as the Confederacy's Attorney General, Secretary of War, and Secretary of State, and, despite his intermarriage and complete lack of personal religious observance, always acknowledged his Judaism and always was known as a Jew.

On the homefront, too, Jews in Washington and across the country actively supported their comrades in arms. Men contributed thousands of dollars to relief activities. Women sewed clothes, prepared bandages, tended the wounded, staffed booths and tables at "sanitary fairs," and collected funds for the needy.

Whatever pride Jews took in the military and civilian achievements of their fellow Jews was offset by the sadness, anger, and bewilderment engendered by the sectional cleavage, especially as it pitted Jew against Jew and family members against one another. As the invading Northern armies moved into the South, such problems multiplied. One Southern Jew found his house guarded by two Jewish soldiers from Ohio. "They felt very sorry for us," he recalled, "but could afford us no help." Another memoirist related the stir that took place when Northern soldiers attended worship services at the synagogue in Natchez, Mississippi. Still another account – this one in a contemporary letter – described how frightened some local Jews in Memphis, Tennessee, became when Colonel Spiegel of Ohio, dressed in full Northern military regalia, wished them a "Happy Sabbath" and inquired as to where he might find a kosher lunch.

Maintaining traditional Jewish observances under wartime conditions proved immensely difficult, though commensurately satisfying for those who lived up to the challenge. Two brothers named Levy who fought for the Confederacy reputedly "observed their religion faithfully . . . never even eating forbidden food." The awe with which this was recounted at the time that one of the brothers was killed suggests that such scrupulousness was extremely rare. The same was true of the Northern soldier who described for readers of *The Jewish Messenger* how Jewish men in his outfit met for worship each Saturday on the outskirts of their camp in the Virginia forests. More commonly, Jewish soldiers strove to observe Judaism's major annual holidays, notably Rosh Hashanah and Yom Kippur in the fall as well as Passover in the spring. One Jewish soldier planned to journey twelve miles to attend High Holiday services in Norfolk, Virginia, then in Union hands. Two years later, Jews stationed near Vicksburg, Mississippi, elected a young rabbi, Max del Banco, to conduct High Holiday services especially for them. The unfortunate rabbi was killed in a steamboat accident on his way back home. Many other soldiers received passes for the holidays. General Robert E. Lee, himself a committed Christian, pledged in 1864 to do all in his power "to facilitate the observance of the duties of their religion by the Israelites in the army," and to allow them "every indulgence consistent with safety and discipline."

We possess two lengthy accounts, one from the Union and one from the Confederacy, concerning the observance of Passover in 1862 – a sure sign of how significant commemoration of the holiday of freedom was to Jews on both sides of the struggle. The Southern soldiers purchased the requisite *matzo* in Charleston and cooked a fine traditional dinner, complete with "a pound and a half of fresh kosher beef." The Northern soldiers, stationed in West Virginia, obtained from Cincinnati some of the supplies that they needed for their *seder*, and then went out and foraged for the rest. "We consecrated and offered up to the ever-loving God of Israel our prayers and sacrifice. . . ," one of the participants recalled four years later, "there is no occasion in my life that gives me more pleasure and satisfaction then [sic] when I remember the celebration of Passover of 1862."

Given the strong evangelical character of some Civil War units and the rapidity with which some Jews had abandoned Jewish practices following their immigration, it comes as no surprise that the Civil War also found many Jews who, while serving as soldiers, hid their Jewish identities, maintaining no Jewish rituals whatsoever. Isaac Leeser, who in 1864 visited soldiers recovering from wounds, found that some "would scarcely confess their Jewish origin" and "even refused prayer-books when tendered to them." In the military as in civilian life, American Judaism thus covered a broad spectrum, embracing the meticulously observant, the totally non-observant, and all points in between.

Two extraordinary episodes distinguished the Northern Jewish experience during the Civil War, both of long-lasting significance. The first was the battle to amend the military chaplaincy law, passed in 1861, which stipulated that a regimental chaplain be "a regular ordained minister of some Christian denomination." An amendment to substitute the more inclusive phrase "of some religious society" had been voted down; significantly, the Confederate law, which employed the phrase "minister of religion," was more inclusive.

Protestant chaplains and – to the extent that they could – Catholics made the most of their opportunities to exert a religious influence on warring troops. At their best, these chaplains tended to soldiers' spiritual needs, helped them to overcome personal and family problems, and modeled virtuous and courageous behavior under fire. Jewish chaplains, by contrast, were officially barred from the field, greatly disadvantaging Jewish soldiers and, in effect, delegitimizing the Jewish faith.

At least two elected Jewish chaplains (one of whom was not "regularly ordained") were rejected on account of the discriminatory law, setting off a national debate involving Christians and Jews alike. Although many supported a change in the law, one evangelical paper complained that if the law were changed, "one might despise and reject the Savior of men . . . and yet be a fit minister of religion." It warned that "Mormon debauchees, Chinese priests, and Indian conjurors" would stand next in line for government recognition – a tacit admission that the central issue under debate concerned the religious rights of non-Christians.

To further the Jewish cause, one of the rejected chaplains, Rev. Arnold Fischel, came to Washington at the behest of the Board of Delegates of American Israelites to lobby personally on behalf of a change in the chaplaincy law, and President Lincoln promised him support. After substantial wrangling, a revised bill that construed "some Christian denomination" in the original legislation to read "some religious denomination" became law on July 17, 1862. This represented a major political victory for the Jewish community and remains a landmark in the legal recognition of America's non-Christian faiths. In this case, as in so many others, American religious liberty was broadened by the demands of those who stood outside the American religious mainstream.

The second episode involving Jews was far uglier. On December 17, 1862, a general order went out from Ulysses S. Grant's headquarters in Oxford, Mississippi, which read as follows:

> 1. The Jews, as a class, violating every regulation of trade established by the Treasury Department, and also Department orders, are hereby expelled from the Department.
>
> 2. Within twenty-four hours from the receipt of this order by Post Commanders, they will see that all of this class of people are furnished with passes and required to leave, and any one returning after such notification, will be arrested and held in confinement until an opportunity occurs of sending them out as prisoners unless furnished with permits from these Head Quarters.
>
> 3. No permits will be given these people to visit Head Quarters for the purpose of making personal application for trade permits.
>
> By Order of Maj. Gen. U.S. Grant

Known as "the most sweeping anti-Jewish legislation in all American history," General Orders No. 11, as it came to be called, blamed "Jews, as a class" for the widespread smuggling and cotton speculation that affected the entire area under Grant's command. Numbers of Jews in Northern Mississippi and Paducah, Kentucky, were forcibly expelled as a result of the order; some were refused rail transportation and had to travel on foot, and at least one was briefly jailed.

Historians have since determined that "Jews were neither the most numerous nor the most iniquitous of the legion of sharpers following the army: their peccadilloes were certainly no greater than the misdeeds of any number of crooked Yankees, Treasury agents and army officers." Indeed, a group of Cincinnati Jewish merchants formed a cotton speculating partnership with Grant's own father, Jesse Grant. At the time, however, Jews were "easily identifiable by their manners, accents, and surnames," and also stigmatized by age-old stereotypes, so that they came to symbolize *all* who were attempting to profit from wartime speculation and cross-border trading. The tensions and frustrations of war, which elsewhere found their outlet in persecutions of Catholics and African Americans, were directed – in this case – at "Jews as a class."

For their part, Jews lost no time in protesting Grant's order. Not only did they send letters and telegrams to the White House, but one of those expelled, Cesar Kaskel of Paducah, Kentucky, rushed to Washington and, accompanied by Cincinnati's Congressman John A. Gurley, went directly to President Lincoln's office. The President turned out to know nothing of the order, which he had never seen. According to a revealing but unverifiable later tradition, he resorted to biblical imagery in his interview with Kaskel, a reminder of how many 19th-century Americans linked Jews to Ancient Israel and America to the Promised Land:

> Lincoln: And so the children of Israel were driven from the happy land of Canaan?
>
> Kaskel: Yes, and that is why we have come unto Father Abraham's bosom, asking protection.
>
> Lincoln: And this protection they shall have at once.

Even if no such conversation actually took place, Lincoln did instantly command the General-in-Chief of the Army, Henry Halleck, to countermand General Orders No. 11. "If such an order has been issued," Halleck telegraphed Grant on January 4, 1863, "it will be immediately revoked." In a follow-up meeting with Jewish leaders, including Rabbis Wise and Lilienthal, who had rushed to Washington to support Kaskel, Lincoln reiterated that "to condemn a class is, to say the least, to wrong the good with the bad. I do not like to hear a class or nationality condemned on account of a few sinners." After a few weeks of recriminations and a failed move by Congressional opponents to censure Grant, the whole issue blew over.

Its implications, though, were profound. On the one hand, the episode reminded Jews that hoary prejudices against them remained alive – even in America. In fact, a dramatic upsurge in many forms of anti-Jewish intolerance, in the North as well as in the South, characterized the Civil War era, Grant's order being the most notorious but far from the only example. On the other hand, the episode also empowered Jews with the knowledge that they could fight back against bigotry and win – even against a prominent general. The overturning of Grant's order, especially on top of the victory in the chaplaincy affair, appreciably strengthened the Jewish community and increased its self-confidence. The successes also validated an activist Jewish communal policy that based claims to equality on American law and values while relying on help from public officials to combat prejudice and defend Jews' minority rights.

The surrender of Confederate General-in-Chief Robert E. Lee at Appomattox Court House on April 9, 1865, coincided with final preparations for the eight-day Jewish holiday of Passover. Throughout the North that Passover, Jews gave thanks for the redemption of their ancestors from slavery in Egypt and for the restoration of peace to the inhabitants of the United States. The calendrical link between the anniversary of the biblical Exodus and the victory of the Union forces seemed to the faithful almost providential.

The assassination of Abraham Lincoln, five days after the surrender, came on the eve of the fifth day of Passover (coinciding that year with Good Friday) and was harder for Jews to reconcile with the holiday spirit. Synagogues the next morning were filled with grief-stricken worshippers, and mournful melodies replaced the customary Passover ones. In subsequent sermons delivered in Lincoln's memory by rabbis across the United States, the President was compared to the patriarch Abraham, to King David, and above all to Moses, who died without entering the Promised Land. Isaac Leeser delivered the memorial address on April 22nd at Washington Hebrew Congregation.

Southern Judaism became increasingly distinctive during the post-Civil War decades. As an example, Jews in Southern cities turned out together as a community to celebrate Confederate Memorial Day and set aside special sections of their cemeteries for Confederate War victims. The distinguished Jewish sculptor Moses Ezekiel, himself a Confederate veteran and a loyal Southerner (even though he lived in Rome), abetted this cult of martyrdom. He produced a whole series of "Lost Cause" monuments, including the "New South" monument to the Confederate War dead at Arlington

National Cemetery, five busts of Robert E. Lee, a large bronze statue of Stonewall Jackson, and a monument entitled *Virginia Mourning Her Dead*. In his autobiography, Ezekiel described the latter in religious terms ("one of the most sacred duties in my life") and explains that he wanted it to serve as a memorial to his fallen comrades, "sounding their heroism and Virginia's memory down through all ages and forever." While Northern Jews put the war behind them and moved on, Southern Jews, like their neighbors, thus made the Lost Cause the centerpiece of their faith. Focusing on the martyrdom of lost sons, they insisted that the cause that so many had fought and died for was right.

Washington, D.C., as this book demonstrates, was transformed by the Civil War. Its population, including its Jewish population, multiplied, and on July 31, 1863, Washington Hebrew Congregation dedicated its first synagogue, formerly the Methodist Episcopal church on Eighth Street. The war years also witnessed the establishment of a Hebrew elementary school, a Jewish "Literary and Dramatic Association," and a new B'nai B'rith Lodge, Elijah Lodge No. 50.

Simon Wolf, a precocious 27-year-old Jewish lawyer in the city, recorded "a favorable change in the condition of the Jewish residents in the capital of the nation," in 1864. By the end of the Civil War, the Washington Jewish community was firmly established and poised to grow.

AUTHOR'S NOTE: For additional information on Washington, D.C., during this period, see Robert Shosteck, "The Jewish Community of Washington, D.C., during the Civil War," *American Jewish Historical Quarterly* 56 (March 1957), 319-347, which is also condensed beginning on page 113 of this volume.

JEWISH LIFE IN MR. LINCOLN'S CITY

Text and Images From the Exhibition

A HOUSE DIVIDED

"THE CAPITOL, WITH ITS UNFINISHED DOME AND INCOMPLETE WINGS, PRESENT BUT AN IMPERFECT PICTURE OF WHAT ITS APPEARANCE IS ULTIMATELY DESTINED TO BE."

- A Jewish Soldier,
"A Tour of Washington City"
The Jewish Messenger

When the Civil War broke out on April 12, 1861, the United States split between North and South. President Abraham Lincoln led the Union from the nation's capital, just across the river from Confederate Alexandria, Virginia.

Nearly 25,000 of the nation's 150,000 Jews lived in Confederate states. Over 8,000 Jews joined the fight on both sides.

In Washington and in Union-occupied Alexandria, members of the Jewish community—many of them recent immigrants—responded to the bloody conflict in diverse ways.

At Abraham Lincoln's first inauguration on March 4, 1861, the Capitol dome was still unfinished. Five weeks later, the Civil War broke out.

View of Alexandria, 1863.

Between August 1861 and March 1862, an anonymous individual identified as "A Jewish Soldier" wrote "Sketches from the Seat of War," a series of articles for *The Jewish Messenger,* a weekly newspaper based in New York City.

FROM THE CITY OF WASHINGTON, ALEXANDRIA IS REACHED BY WRETCHED FERRY BOATS FROM THE FOOT OF SEVENTH STREET, WHERE MILITARY OFFICERS ARE STATIONED TO EXAMINE THE PASSPORTS.

– A Jewish Soldier,
"Alexandria, Virginia, and its Jewish population"
The Jewish Messenger

THE

JEWISH MESSENGER

Vol. 13. מבשר טוב משמיע ישועה No.

"A MESSENGER OF GOOD TIDINGS, PUBLISHING SALVATION."

NEW YORK, SHEVAT 17, 5623, FEBRUARY 6, 1863.

The Jewess of Toledo!
TALE OF THE FIFTEENTH CENTURY

usual custom, with a kiss upon the cheek, he was surprised to find the maiden shrink back, and avert her head, as though the act he meditated was both unwelcome and presumptuous.
Ezra Martinez and Zillah exchanged significant glan

sullied honor, I might have attributed to arise fr love, somewhat different from that which should between a brother and sister."
Raphael started, and become visibly agitated, a eyes once more encountered those of the old man pe

A CITY TRANSFORMED

"...ON ENTERING THE CAPITAL, YOU FEEL THAT YOU ARE INDEED APPROACHING THE SCENES OF ACTUAL CONFLICT; A COMPANY OF SOLDIERS, WITH GLISTENING BAYONETS, RECEIVE YOU AT THE STATION; STRONG PATROLS GO TO AND FRO THROUGH THE STREETS, TO PICK UP STRAY SOLDIERS AND OFFICERS..."

–A Jewish Soldier,
"Four Hundred Thousand Men"
The Jewish Messenger

For the Union, Washington was the wartime hub. Over 30,000 soldiers were dispatched to forts encircling the city. Federal buildings, schools, and churches were converted to barracks and hospitals. Battles raged nearby in Manassas, Virginia (1861 & 1862), and Frederick, Maryland (1862).

War brought the city unexpected prosperity. Skyrocketing prices and demand for food, lodging, and household goods enriched merchants, tailors, and boarding-house operators. Six kosher restaurants were among the more than 450 restaurants operating in the city during the Civil War.

Union forces pose in front of the unfinished Washington Monument on what would become the National Mall.

When President Lincoln visited Fort Stevens on July 12, 1864, he was the first sitting U.S. president to come under fire—at the only battle fought within the city's lines. Among the Union defenders during the two-day battle were Jewish members of the 122nd New York Volunteer Infantry, including Max Friedlander, Israel Mannheimer, and Jacob Sax. The battle ended in Union victory.

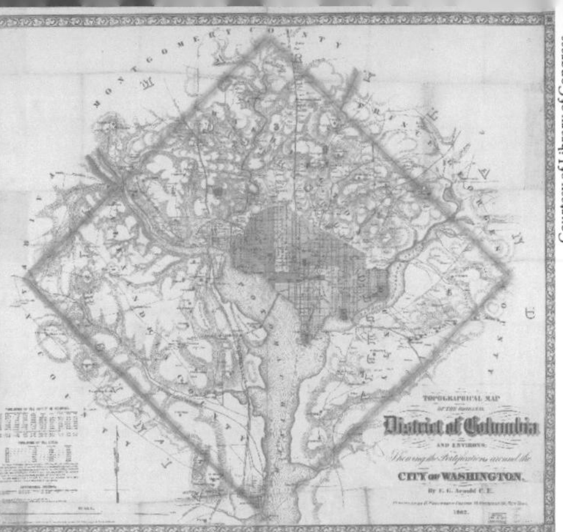

Courtesy of Library of Congress

A protective ring of forts was built around Washington in an effort to keep the capital city safe, because of its proximity to Southern states.

SLAVERY IN THE CAPITAL CITY

Although the Compromise of 1850 had banned the slave trade in the District of Columbia, those already enslaved remained so. By 1860 there were just over 3,000 slaves in Washington. Several Jews owned slaves.

On April 16, 1862, nine months before the Emancipation Proclamation, President Lincoln signed The District of Columbia Emancipation Act, freeing all slaves in the city.

SCHEDULE 2.—Slave Inhabitants in the 2nd Ward City of Washington in the County of Washington of D.C., enumerated by me, on the 8th day of July, 1850. [illegible]

Names of Slave Owners	Number of Slaves	Age	Sex	Colour	Fugitives from the State	Number manumitted	Deaf & dumb, blind, insane, or idiotic
1	2	3	4	5	6	7	8
Jos. I. Wilson	1	20	F	B			
"	2	15	M	B			
Wm Dowling	1	40	F	M			
Richd. Burgess	1	12	M	M			
J. B. Waugh	1	15	M	B			
J. S. Reed	1	42	M	B			
"	2	45	M	B			
S. H. Hobbie	1	40	F	B			
"	2	22	F	M			
"	3	9	F	B			
"	4	7	M	M			
B. M. Reed	1	18	F	B			
"	2	14	M	B			
"	3	12	F	M			
A. Butler	1	61	F	B			
M. Manning	1	26	M	M			
"	2	14	F	B			
C. Liebermann	1	29	F	B			
"	2	15	M	B			
"	3	12	M	M			
Elvira Simms	1	27	F	B			
"	2	10	F	M			
S. K. Ferris	1	42	F	M			
R. K. Stone	1	21	M	B			
"	2	35	F	B			
T. O. Patten	1	26	F	B			
I. C. Henshaw	1	56	M	B			
"	2	56	F	B			
"	3	21	F	B			
"	4	17	M	B			
"	5	6	F	M			
J. M. Cutts	1	23	F	B			
"	2	1	F	B			
"	3	1/2	M	B			
Dr. Causin	1	35	F	B			
Henry Hungerford	1	18	F	B			
R. B. Kirkpatrick	1	10	F	M			
"	2	20	F	B			

Names of Slave Owners	Number of Slaves	Age	Sex	Colour	Fugitives from the State
1	2	3	4	5	6
"	3	55	F	B	
"	4	33	F	B	
"	5	15	M	B	
"	6	23	M	M	
"	7	45	F	M	
James Riordan	1	14	F	B	
C. T. Gardner	1	25	F	B	
"	2	5	F	M	
[illegible]	1	9	F	B	
Jacob [illegible]	1	25	F	M	
"	2	24	F	M	
H. O. Heiskell	1	10	M	M	
W. T. Swann	1	16	F	M	
David Finch	1	30	F	B	
O. B. [illegible] Hazard	1	3	M	B	
"	2	9	F	B	
"	3	6	F	B	
"	4	26	F	M	
"	5	56	F	B	
A. Sailor	1	40	F	B	
"	2	20	M	B	
"	3	24	M	B	
"	4	10	M	B	
"	5	8	F	B	
"	6	2	M	B	
C. Alexander	1	65	F	B	
"	2	28	F	B	
Ann Graham	1	70	F	B	
"	2	30	M	B	
"	3	29	F	B	
"	4	8	F	B	
T. R. Peale	1	29	F	B	
Wm Miller	1	26	F	M	
"	2	22	F	M	
"	3	8	F	M	
"	4	8	F	B	
"	5	2	M	M	
Henry E. [illegible]	1	[illegible]	[illegible]	[illegible]	

This document is used with permission of Ancestry.com.

This slave census from 1850 shows that Dr. Charles Liebermann, a Russian-born immigrant, owned three slaves ranging in age from 12 to 29.

Courtesy of Library of Congress

Until 1850, Washington had one of the largest slave depots in the nation. Slaves for sale passed through the city in shackles, within view of the Capitol.

A CAPITAL COMMUNITY

"THE REV. S. WEIL RECITE[D] THE PRAYER FOR THE GOVERNMENT IN BOTH HEBREW AND ENGLISH... THE CONGREGATION IS PROSPERING GREATLY, NUMBERING ABOUT NINETY MEMBERS."

-*The Jewish Messenger,* December 11, 1863

WASHINGTON HEBREW CONGREGATION

Washington Hebrew Congregation cared for Jewish soldiers and buried Jews whose bodies went unclaimed. A corps of congregation women raised money to benefit the U.S. Sanitary Commission's wartime relief work.

Initially rooted in Orthodox practice, changes in ritual began by 1861. Reforms included eliminating the second day of holidays, using a cornet for a *shofar*, and adopting Rabbi Isaac Mayer Wise's prayer book, *Minhag America*.

Washington, D.C., in 1861. Note that the Capitol dome is still under construction.

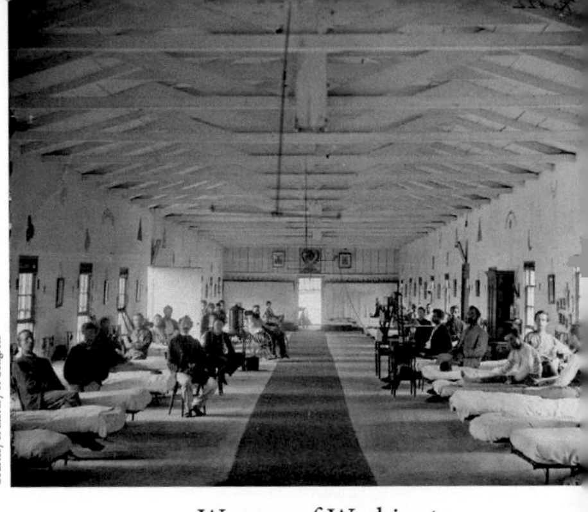

Courtesy of Library of Congress

Women of Washington Hebrew Congregation tended to wounded soldiers in local wartime hospitals such as this one at Armory Square at Independence Avenue and Seventh Street, SW.

During the Civil War Washington's Jewish population grew from 200 to nearly 2,000. The only Jewish congregation, Washington Hebrew, was made up primarily of German-speaking immigrant merchants and clerks. Most lived and worked in the Seventh Street, NW, neighborhood.

Social clubs like Harmonie Circle and Select Assembly provided fellowship through masked Purim balls and other soirees. When Elijah Lodge No. 5 opened in 1864, it signaled the arrival of the Independent Order of B'nai B'rith.

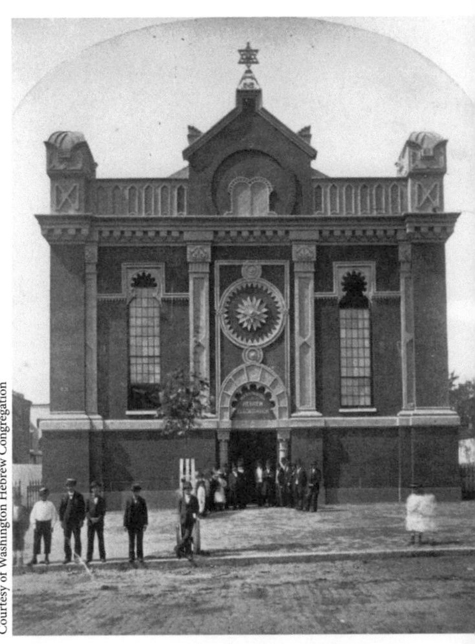

Courtesy of Washington Hebrew Congregation

Washington Hebrew Congregation purchased this former Methodist church at Eighth and I Streets, NW, in 1863, and converted it to synagogue use during the Civil War.

...SGW Collections

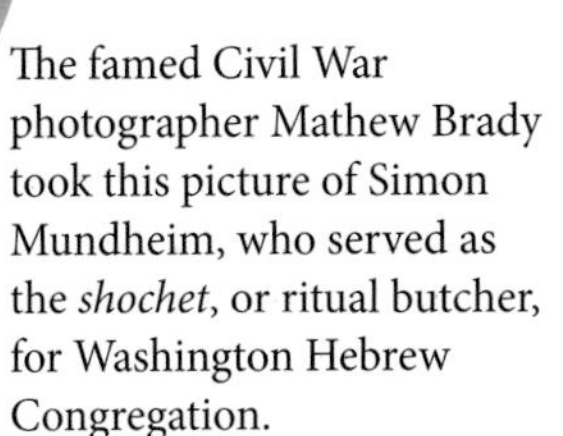

The famed Civil War photographer Mathew Brady took this picture of Simon Mundheim, who served as the *shochet*, or ritual butcher, for Washington Hebrew Congregation.

Columbia

Wöchentliches Unterhaltungsblatt.

Herausgegeben und redigirt von Max Cohnheim.

[1. Jahrgang.] Washington, D. C., Samstag, den 13. Februar 1864.

Courtesy of Library of Congress

German immigrant Max Cohnheim edited and published a weekly German-language newspaper, *Columbia*. Starting with 200 readers in 1863, it grew to more than 1,600 by 1865.

CIVIL WAR MERCHANTS

Many Jewish Washingtonians during the Civil War operated small businesses, particularly along Seventh Street, NW. Some of these establishments grew to become prominent in the Washington community.

In the early 1860s, brothers Gustav and Max Lansburgh opened Baltimore House, a small fancy goods store on C Street, NW. It was the predecessor to the landmark Lansburgh's Department Store on Seventh Street, NW.

LIFE ACROSS THE RIVER

On May 24, 1861, just over a month after the war began, Union forces occupied Alexandria, Virginia, to secure the heights overlooking the Potomac River and establish a buffer zone between Confederate Virginia and the capital city. Alexandria quickly became a large personnel and medical center for the United States Army.

Alexandria's Jewish community numbered between 30 to 40 families at the start of the war but soon grew to more than 300. Jewish-owned shops and homes were located in the city's most well-traveled area, along King Street between Royal and Washington Streets.

"IN THE PRINCIPAL BUSINESS STREET, I COULD EASILY IDENTIFY HALF THE FIRMS AS BELONGING TO THE WELL-KNOWN JEWISH NOMENCLATURE; TWO KOSHER BOARDING-HOUSES ARE ALREADY ESTABLISHED THERE."

- A Jewish Soldier,
"Alexandria, Virginia, and its Jewish Population"
The Jewish Messenger

Occupying Union soldiers at Alexandria's City Hall on Royal Street, 1863.

Courtesy of Alexandria Library, Special Collections

View of Union-occupied Alexandria, 1864

BETH EL HEBREW CONGREGATION, ALEXANDRIA, VIRGINIA

Formed in 1859, Beth El Hebrew Congregation followed reform traditions, conducted services in German and Hebrew, and used Rabbi Isaac Mayer Wise's prayer book *Minhag America*.

From the early 1860s until 1871, members held services in a rented room at the corner of King and Pitt Streets. In 1864, the congregation hired its first spiritual leader, Dr. L. Schlessinger.

"THE MOST SACRED OF THE HEBREW FEASTS BEGAN YESTERDAY EVENING . . . THE STORES OF ALL THE JEWS IN THE CITY HAVE BEEN CLOSED SINCE YESTERDAY EVENING AT 6:00 P.M."

-Excerpt from *The Gazette*

The Alexandria Gazette

WEDNESDAY EVENING, SEPT'R. 23.

YOM KIPPUR.—The most sacred of the Hebrew feasts began yesterday evening, and will continue until this evening. It is known among the people of that faith, who strictly observe it, as a day of atonement for sin. No manual labor is permitted, and they faithfully abstain from all food and drink. In consequence of the fast, the stores of all the Jews in the city have been closed since yesterday evening at 6 o'clock, and will so remain until 6 o'clock this evening.

Courtesy Alexandria Public Library, Special Collections

The *Alexandria Gazette* reported activities of Beth El Hebrew Congregation during Yom Kippur in 1863.

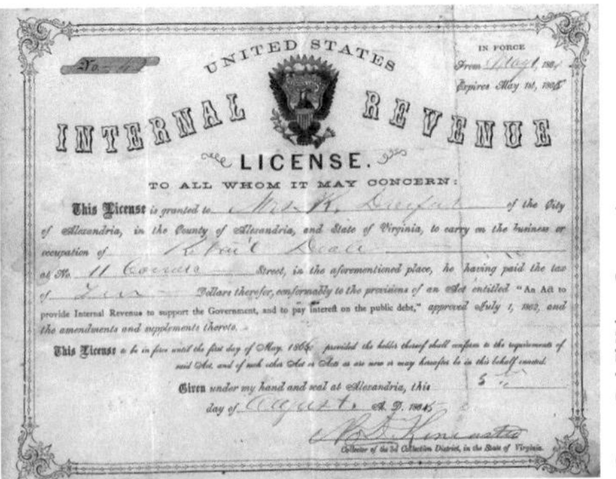

UNITED STATES INTERNAL REVENUE LICENSE.

IN FORCE From May 1, 1864 Expires May 1st, 1865

TO ALL WHOM IT MAY CONCERN:

This License is granted to Mrs. K. Dreifus of the City of Alexandria, in the County of Alexandria, and State of Virginia, to carry on the business or occupation of Retail Dealer at No. 11 Commerce Street, in the aforementioned place, he having paid the tax of Ten Dollars therefor, conformably to the provisions of an Act entitled "An Act to provide Internal Revenue to support the Government, and to pay interest on the public debt," approved July 1, 1862, and the amendments and supplements thereto.

This License to be in force until the first day of May, 1865 provided the holder thereof shall conform to the requirements of said Act, and of such other Act or Acts as are now or may hereafter be in this behalf enacted.

Given under my hand and seal at Alexandria, this 5 day of August, A. D. 1864

Collector of the 3d Collection District, in the State of Virginia.

Courtesy Beth El Hebrew Congregation

An 1865 business license issued to Caroline Dreifus as a "retail dealer" at 11 Commerce Street. Caroline Dreifus was the widow of Simpson Dreifus, a founding member of the congregation.

JHSGW Collections, gift of Martin Baum and Evelyn Conn

The *ketubah*, or marriage contract, for Bettie Dreifus and Henry Baum, 1862.

A WARTIME WEDDING

In 1862, when it was clear the war would not end quickly, President Lincoln issued a draft for the Union army. Travel restrictions prevented eligible men from leaving their home states to avoid the draft.

That same year, 26-year-old Bettie Dreifus of Alexandria planned to marry Washington's Henry Baum. Because of the new travel prohibitions, the groom could not travel to his bride's home in Alexandria. So the couple married in Washington.

CONFEDERATE TIES

Many Alexandrians sympathized with the Confederacy. When occupying Union forces required local businessmen to take a loyalty oath, several initially refused, including shoe-store owner Joseph Rosenthal and clothing-store owner Simon Waterman.

Military officers ordered several merchants thought to be disloyal, including Waterman, to be transported from the city in June 1863. After the Secretary of War rescinded the order, Waterman signed an Oath of Loyalty to the Union on July 9, 1863.

xample of a loyalty oath:

_______ of the County of _________, State of _________, do solemnly
,ear, in presence of Almighty God, that I will henceforth faithfully
pport, protect, and defend the Constitution of the United States, and
e Union of the States thereunder; and that I will, in like manner, abide
' and faithfully support all acts of Congress passed during the existing
bellion with reference to slaves, so long and so far as not repealed,
odified, or held void by Congress, or by decision of the Supreme Court;
d that I will, in like manner, abide by and faithfully support all
oclamations of the President made during the existing rebellion having
ference to slave, so long and so far as not modified or declared void by
cision of the Supreme Court: So help me God.

_______________________________ (signature)

bscribed and sworn to before me, at ____________this _____
y of ____, A.D. 186___.

ie above-named has _____ complexion, ______ hair, and _____ eyes; and
____ feet _____ inches high.

THAT OBNOXIOUS ORDER

Courtesy of Library of Congress

In 1864, President Lincoln appointed General Ulysses S. Grant General-in-Chief of the Union forces. Grant, shown here on the battlefield at Cold Harbor, Virginia, led the Union to victory in 1865.

On December 17, 1862, Major General Ulysses S. Grant issued General Orders No.11, expelling Jews "as a class" from the Department of the Tennessee—an area under his command that included parts of southern Illinois, Kentucky, and Mississippi. Blaming Jewish traders for the black market sale of Southern cotton across Union lines, Grant gave Jews —men, women, and children— twenty-four hours to leave.

As word of the outrage spread and Jews were evicted from their homes, Jewish communal leaders rushed to respond.

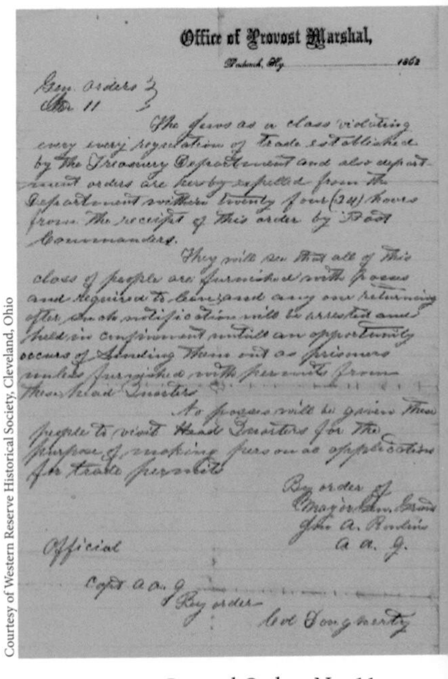

Office of Provost Marshal,

Paducah, Ky. 1862

Gen. Orders
No. 11

The Jews as a class violating every every regulation of trade established by the Treasury Department and also department orders are hereby expelled from the Department within twenty four (24) hours from the receipt of this order by Post Commanders.

They will see that all of this class of people are furnished with passes and required to leave, and any one returning after such notification will be arrested and held in confinement untill an opportunity occurs of sending them out as prisoners unless furnished with permits from these Head Quarters.

No passes will be given these people to visit Head Quarters for the purpose of making personal application for trade permits.

By order of
Major Gen. Grant
Jno. A. Rawlins
A. A. G.

Official

Capt A. A. G.
By order
Col Dougherty

Courtesy of Western Reserve Historical Society, Cleveland, Ohio

General Orders No. 11, which expelled Jews from areas under General Grant's command in the west.

"IN THE NAME OF THAT CLASS OF LOYAL CITIZENS OF THESE U. S. WHICH WE IN PART REPRESENT... IN THE NAME OF HUNDREDS WHO HAVE BEEN DRIVEN FROM THEIR HOMES, DEPRIVED OF THEIR LIBERTY AND INJURED IN THEIR PROPERTY WITHOUT HAVING VIOLATED ANY LAW OR REGULATION . . ."

-Letter from B'nai B'rith Missouri Lodge President Henry Kuttner in St. Louis to President Abraham Lincoln, January 5, 1863

Courtesy of B'nai B'rith Klutznick National Jewish Museum

Cesar Kaskel led a delegation from Paducah, Kentucky, to entreat the President to rescind Grant's order.

THE RESPONSE

Hundreds of angry letters, many from B'nai B'rith chapters, reached President Lincoln's desk in late December. Cesar Kaskel of Paducah, Kentucky, led a Jewish delegation to meet with the President. During the meeting, Kaskel explained how long-time residents of the Jewish community in Paducah, including two Union army veterans, were given just 24 hours to leave their homes. Lincoln wrote to General-in-Chief of the Army, Henry Halleck, to have General Orders No. 11 immediately rescinded.

United Order "Bne B'rith" Missouri Loge
St Louis. Jan 5' 1863.

To his Excellency
Abr. Lincoln
President U. S.

Sir

An Order, Expelling and Ostracising all Jews, as a class has been issued by Maj. Genl U. S. Grant and has been Enforced at Holly Springs, Trenton, Corinth, Paducah, Jackson and other places.—

In the name of that Class of loyal citizens of these U. S. which we in part represent.

In the name of hundreds, who have been driven from their homes, deprived of their liberty and injured in their property without having violated any laws or regulation.

In the name of the thousands of our Brethren and our children who have died and are now willingly sacrificing their lives and fortunes for the Union and the suppression of this rebellion

In the name of religious liberty, of justice and humanity — we Enter our Solemn Protest against this Order, and ask of you — the Defendor & Protector of the Constitution — to annull that Order and to protect the liberties Even of your humblest Constituents

Morris Hoffman
Secy

Henry. Kuttner
President

Courtesy of B'nai B'rith Klutznick National Jewish Museum

Henry Kuttner, President of the Missouri Lodge of B'nai B'rith, wrote to President Lincoln asserting that the Jews were a class of "loyal citizens."

POSTSCRIPT

During his 1868 campaign for the presidency, General Orders No. 11 haunted Grant. While he never publicly apologized for the decision, he referred privately to it as "that obnoxious order."

In 1876, Grant attended the dedication of Adas Israel synagogue in Washington, D.C. He remained for the entire three-hour service and made a ten-dollar donation to the synagogue's building fund.

Courtesy of Smithsonian Institution

As president from 1869 to 1877, Ulysses S. Grant worked to mend his relationship with American Jews. He paid attention to mistreatment of Jews in Romania and Russia. In 1870, he appointed Benjamin Franklin Peixotto, Grand Master of B'nai B'rith, as Consul to Bucharest, Romania.

Courtesy of Washingtoniana Division, DC Public Library

Grant attended the dedication of Adas Israel's first synagogue, making him the first U.S. president at a synagogue service.

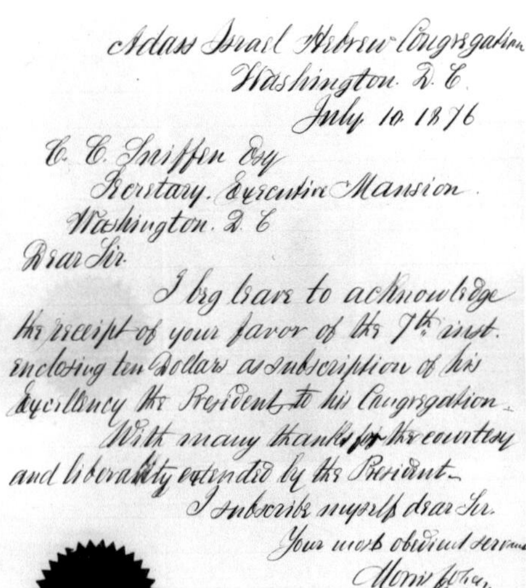

Adas Israel Hebrew Congregation
Washington D.C.
July 10 1876

C. C. Sniffen Esq
Secretary. Executive Mansion
Washington D.C
Dear Sir

I beg leave to acknowledge the receipt of your favor of the 7th inst. enclosing ten Dollars as subscription of his Excellency the President to his Congregation.

With many thanks for the courtesy and liberality extended by the President

I subscribe myself dear Sir
Your most obedient servant
Morris Cohen,
Secty.

Courtesy of Ulysses S. Grant Papers, Library of Congress

This receipt from Adas Israel Congregation acknowledges Grant's ten-dollar donation to the synagogue building fund.

JUBILATION AND SORROW

"After the surrender of General Lee, the City of Washington was illuminated on the night of the twelfth of April, 1865. In passing down H Street, between Sixth and Seventh, I noticed that one house was dark and not illuminated. It turned out to have been the house of Mrs. Surratt, who was hung as one of the conspirators in the plot to assassinate the President."

- Simon Wolf, *Presidents I have Known,* 1921 [Wolf recalled this strange occurrence a few nights before Lincoln's assassination]

Jubilant celebrations marked the Confederate surrender on April 9, 1865. But the thrill of victory was cut short. On Friday, April 14, after Jews had ushered in the Sabbath and the fifth day of Passover, John Wilkes Booth assassinated President Lincoln at Ford's Theatre. The nation mourned.

During the war, Washington's population grew to 140,000, nearly double that of the 1860 census. The capital city was evolving into a major metropolis, and Washington's Jewish community would grow and flourish as well.

Courtesy of Library of Congress

Mary Surratt's boarding house on H Street, NW, where the conspirators in the Lincoln assassination met. Simon Wolf recalled seeing it dark a few nights before the assassination.

Courtesy of Library of Congress

Although not identified in this image of Lincoln's deathbed, news accounts reported that Dr. Charles Liebermann was among the doctors at Lincoln's bedside.

DR. CHARLES LIEBERMANN: AT LINCOLN'S BEDSIDE

The mortally-wounded Lincoln was carried from Ford's Theatre across the street to William Peterson's boarding house. There, several doctors, including Dr. Charles Liebermann, attended the President on his deathbed.

Born in Russia, Charles Liebermann had practiced medicine in Washington since 1840. A successful surgeon and founding member of the Georgetown University medical department, Liebermann was President of the Medical Society of the District of Columbia at the time of Lincoln's assassination.

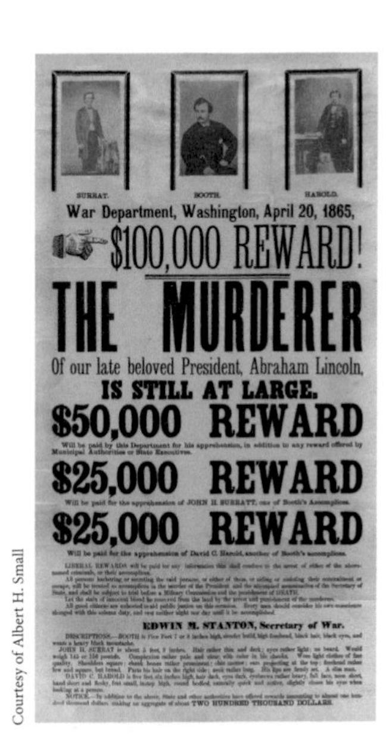

Courtesy of Albert H. Small

Broadside advertising reward for the capture of John Wilkes Booth and his co-conspirators, David Harold and John Surratt.

Philp & Solomons hung this image of President Lincoln and his son Tad in their window in tribute to the fallen President. Above hung a sign reading: "Treason has done its worst."

Courtesy of Washingtoniana Division, DC Public Library

The Lansburgh brothers, owners of the fancy goods store Baltimore House, made a $500 donation towards one of the nation's first monuments to the memory of President Lincoln. The statue still stands at Fourth and D Streets, NW.

JEWISH COMMUNITY MOURNS

Jews shared in the nation's sorrow. Isaac Leeser, *hazzan* (cantor) of Philadelphia's Mikveh Israel and one of the leading Jewish scholars of the day, came to the nation's capital to lead a memorial service at Washington Hebrew. In Alexandria, Rabbi H. Heilbroun officiated at Beth El's memorial service.

President Lincoln's funeral procession from the White House to the Capitol on April 19, 1865, included more than 30,000 mourners.

One hundred twenty-five members of the Washington Hebrew Congregation marched down Pennsylvania Avenue in President Lincoln's funeral procession on April 19, 1865.

THE BLUE *Leopold Karpeles*

JHSGW Collections

MEDAL OF HONOR RECIPIENT (1838-1909)

Leopold Karpeles immigrated from Prague to Texas in 1849. After moving to Massachusetts, he enlisted as a flag-bearer in the Union Army.

Sergeant Karpeles carried regimental colors into more than 14 battles, including Gettysburg. He helped turn the tide of the Battle of the Wilderness by rallying the retreating Union troops. Karpeles was later awarded the Medal of Honor for this bravery, one of the first Jews to receive that honor.

Karpeles became a clerk in the U.S. Postal Department following the war. He is buried in Washington Hebrew's cemetery.

JHSGW Collections, portrait by Mathew Brady Studio

Hannah Mundheim headed Washington Hebrew's visiting nurse corps and visited ailing soldiers. Her daughter, Sara Mundheim, tended to Leopold Karpeles in the hospital. The two fell in love and later married.

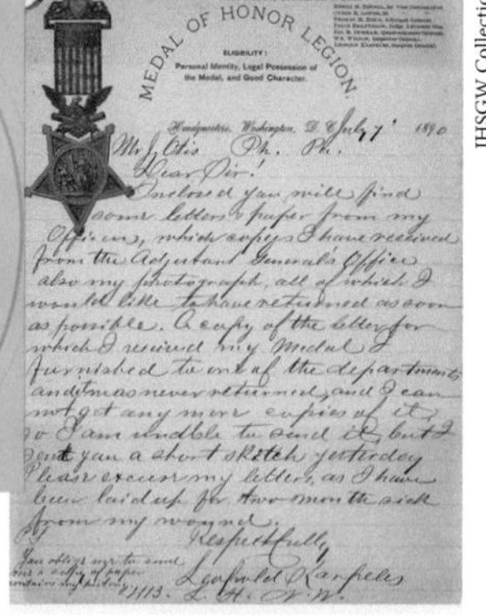

M. A. DILLON, Commander in Chief.

MEDAL OF HONOR LEGION.

ELIGIBILITY: Personal Identity, Legal Possession of the Medal, and Good Character.

Headquarters, Washington, D. C. July 7' 1890

Mr J. Otis Ph. Ph.

Dear Sir!

Inclosed you will find some letters & paper from my Officers, which copies I have received from the Adjutant General's Office also my photograph, all of which I would like to have returned as soon as possible. A copy of the letter for which I received my Medal I furnished to one of the departments and it was never returned, and I can not get any more copies of it, so I am unable to send it, but I sent you a short sketch yesterday. Please excuse my letter, as I have been laid up for two months sick from my wound.

Respectfully,

Leopold Karpeles

JHSGW Collections

In 1890, on the stationery of the newly formed Medal of Honor Legion, Karpeles wrote this letter concerning his military pension.

Courtesy of Library of Congress

Injured in the Battle of North Anna River, Karpeles convalesced at Mount Pleasant Hospital, shown here.

Adajah Behrend

JHSGW Collections, Nordlinger-Behrend-Goldstein Family Archives

HOSPITAL STEWARD

(1841-1932)

Adajah Behrend immigrated to America from Rodenberg in the German state of Hesse. In 1861 he enlisted in the 2nd Regiment Infantry of the U.S. Army and was promoted to Hospital Steward.

Wounded at the James River in 1862, Behrend served until the war's end. After the war, he received his medical degree from Georgetown University, where he later taught, and became a member of Washington Hebrew Congregation. Behrend served as "Physician to the Poor" in northeast Washington.

A FATHER'S PLEA

In November 1862, President Lincoln issued an order allowing soldiers to attend church on Sundays when circumstances permitted. In response, Adajah Behrend's father, Bernhard, wrote to Lincoln. Behrend's letter inquired, "Shall you not give the same privilege to a minority of the army that you give to the majority?"

There is no record of Lincoln's response. However, while serving in a Union hospital at Fairfax Seminary in 1863, Adajah Behrend furloughed (granted leave to) eleven soldiers for the High Holidays.

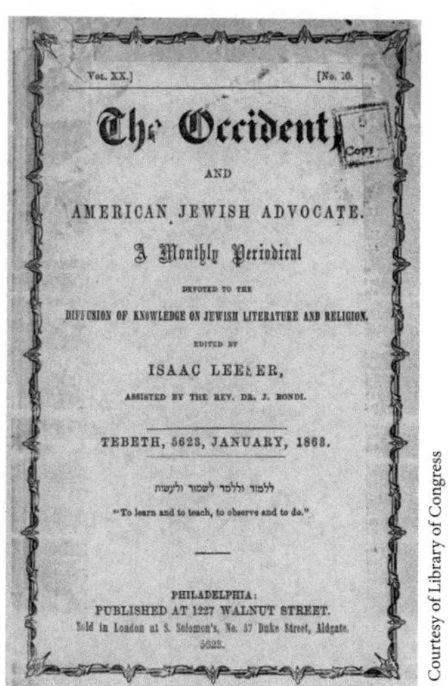

Vol. XX.] [No. 10.

The Occident

AND

AMERICAN JEWISH ADVOCATE.

A Monthly Periodical

DEVOTED TO THE

DIFFUSION OF KNOWLEDGE ON JEWISH LITERATURE AND RELIGION.

EDITED BY

ISAAC LEESER,

ASSISTED BY THE REV. DR. J. BONDI.

TEBETH, 5623, JANUARY, 1863.

ללמוד וללמד לשמור ולעשות

"To learn and to teach, to observe and to do."

PHILADELPHIA:
PUBLISHED AT 1227 WALNUT STREET.
Sold in London at S. Solomon's, No. 37 Duke Street, Aldgate.
5623.

Courtesy of Library of Congress

Bernhard Behrend's letter urging President Lincoln to respect the Jewish Sabbath was published in the Jewish periodical *The Occident*.

THE BLUE *Abraham Hart*

JHSGW Collections, gift of Frank Rich, Sr.

ASSISTANT ADJUTANT GENERAL (1832- 1915)

Born in the German state of Hesse-Darmstadt, Abraham Hart immigrated to Philadelphia in 1850. In 1861 he joined the 73rd Pennsylvania Infantry and was promoted to captain. He was appointed assistant adjutant general—a military administrative officer—before he was wounded in the Second Battle of Bull Run.

After recovering from his wounds in Washington, Hart remained in the city and worked to send supplies to soldiers in the field. After the war he worked as a lawyer and served as commander of the Department of the Potomac, Grand Army of the Republic (a Union veterans' organization).

He is buried at Washington Hebrew Cemetery. Hart's granddaughter, Rosa Frank, married Herbert Rich, owner of Rich's Shoe Store.

Complimentary Reception
by the
Citizens of Washington, D.C.
to the
MEMBERS OF THE
National Encampment,
Grand Army of the Republic,
Thursday evening, September 22 1892
in the
Pension Building.
Committee on
Music, Addresses and Program:
Geo. E. Corson, Chairman, Dr. Frank T. Howe, Secretary,
William Gibson, B. K. Bruce,
John B. Thompson, E. B. Hay,
William B. Pratt.

JHSGW Collections, gift of Frank Rich, Sr.

Abraham Hart's invitation to the 1892 Grand Army of the Republic Encampment at the Pension Building. Union veterans attended annual multi-day gatherings, or encampments, to commemorate their service.

Uriah Phillips Levy

Courtest of Library of Congress

FIRST JEWISH COMMODORE (1792-1862)

Scion of a prominent Philadelphia Jewish family, Uriah Phillips Levy ran away from home at age ten to join the Navy. In 1836, he purchased Thomas Jefferson's home, Monticello. He took command of the Navy's Mediterranean squadron in 1859 and soon became a commodore.

Levy was subjected to six courts-martial for petty offenses. When war broke out in 1861, he visited President Lincoln to offer his services. Lincoln appointed him to the very board that had tried him: the Navy's Court-Martial Board. Levy died four months later.

Captain Jonas Levy

Courtesy of Washington Hebrew Congregation

Uriah Levy's younger brother, naval Captain Jonas Levy, served as president of Washington Hebrew Congregation in 1857. During the Civil War, he declared his loyalty to the South and helped supply goods to the Confederacy.

Eugenia Phillips

Courtesy of Robert Marcus

LEGENDARY SPY

(1819-1902)

Born in Charleston, South Carolina, Eugenia Levy married Philip Phillips, a Jewish lawyer, in 1836. The family moved to Washington in 1853, when Phillips was elected to Congress from Alabama.

After serving one term in Congress, Phillips established a law practice in Washington. He pledged support to the Union. Eugenia was an outspoken supporter of the Confederacy and was suspected of being part of a spy ring run by Rose O'Neal Greenhow. Her support for the Confederacy was so strong that she became known as "a fire-eating secessionist in skirts."

"THIS DAY HAS USHERED IN A NEW ERA IN THE HISTORY OF THE COUNTRY, ONE WHICH MARKS THE ARREST AND IMPRISONMENT OF WOMEN FOR POLITICAL OPINIONS!"

-Excerpt from Eugenia Phillips's diary, August 28, 1861

Courtesy of Library of Congress

After the war, Philip Phillips resumed his law practice, first in New Orleans and later in Washington, D.C. He argued more than 400 cases before the U.S. Supreme Court.

ARRESTED IN WASHINGTON

In August 1861, officials arrested Eugenia and two of her daughters. They were held under house arrest at Rose Greenhow's home, just a few doors from the White House. Eugenia kept a journal during her house arrest.

Former Congressman Phillips eventually secured his family's release on the condition that they head south. The family traveled to Richmond, Virginia. There, Eugenia delivered Union military maps and plans that she had smuggled out of Washington to Confederate President Jefferson Davis.

Courtesy of Washingtoniana Division, DC Public Library

Eugenia Phillips was imprisoned in Rose Greenhow's home at 16th and H Streets, NW.

Courtesy of Library of Congress

Ship Island, a remote barrier island off the coast of Mississippi, served as a prison and detention center for civilians beginning in 1862.

IMPRISONMENT IN LOUISIANA

In 1862, the Phillips family moved to New Orleans. Major General Benjamin "Beast" Butler accused Eugenia of laughing during a Union officer's funeral and teaching her children to spit on Union officers. He banished her to the mosquito-infested Ship Island 65 miles from New Orleans. Eugenia responded: "It has one advantage over the city, sir; you [Butler] will not be there."

Eugenia served 3½ months before returning to New Orleans, where cheering admirers greeted her.

Courtesy of Library of Congress

In Prison
Thursday 28 August 1861
This day has ushered in a new era in the History of the Country one which marks the arrest and imprisonment of women, for political opinions. At eleven oclock we were notified by an officer, that my sister (a visitor) my two daughters and myself were by the

In her diary Eugenia never admits to spying. Entries during her house arrest only detail the daily lives of the imprisoned women. On the day of her arrest, she ordered all of her other private papers destroyed.

 Isaac Schwarz

Courtesy of Beth El Hebrew Congregation

MERCHANT AND SOLDIER (1834-1898)

Isaac Schwarz, a founding member of Beth El Hebrew, was a sergeant with the 17th Virginia Infantry, formed to combat Union advances from Washington. Wounded in the Second Battle of Bull Run, he was honorably discharged and ran a dry goods shop on King Street.

Isaac's brother, Henry Schwarz, placed this ad for his store at 132 King Street in the *Alexandria Gazette* in 1862:

The War has certainly begun. Go to SCHWARZ's you'll see ther is no fun. He'll sell you for 25 cent the 'Panic Envelope', Containing Hose, Handkerchiefs, Mitts, Combs, and Soap.

SOLDIER'S DISCHARGE.

TO ALL WHOM IT MAY CONCERN.

Courtesy of Beth El Hebrew Congregation

Isaac Schwarz's discharge papers from the Confederate Army.

Courtesy of Library of Congress

A Confederate monument erected in 1889 to honor Alexandria's war dead still stands at Prince and South Washington Streets. It marks the site where soldiers like Schwarz gathered to march into battle.

Bernard Nordlinger

Courtesy of Robin Nordlinger Leiman

CONFEDERATE
BUGLER

(1831-1908)

Originally from Strasbourg, France, Bernard Nordlinger immigrated to Georgia in 1858 and served as *hazzan* (cantor) for Congregation Beth Israel in Macon. In 1861 he joined the Macon German Artillery as a bugler. He was wounded in the Second Battle of Bull Run and later imprisoned at Camp Parole near Annapolis.

After the war, Nordlinger owned a shoe store in Georgetown. A founder of the Mt. Sinai Society, a small Georgetown congregation, he later joined Washington Hebrew when the two congregations merged.

THE GRAY *Judah P. Benjamin*

Courtest of Library of Congress

U.S. SENATOR FROM LOUISIANA (1811-1884)

Judah P. Benjamin served as Louisiana's senator from 1852 until the state seceded in 1861. He lived on Lafayette Park and was once given the honor of holding a new Torah scroll at Washington Hebrew Congregation.

After Louisiana's secession, Benjamin became the highest ranking Jew in the Confederate government. President of the Confederacy Jefferson Davis named him Secretary of War in 1862 and Secretary of State in 1863. He became known as the "brains of the Confederacy."

During the war, Benjamin faced antisemitic criticism from both North and South, even though he had abandoned formal Judaism. He fled to England after the war and became a successful barrister.

Courtesy of B'nai B'rith Klutznick National Jewish Museum

Benjamin appeared on the Confederate States's two-dollar bill.

David Levy Yulee

Courtest of Library of Congress

U.S. SENATOR
FROM FLORIDA
(1810-1886)

One of Florida's first senators, David Levy Yulee left Washington when Florida seceded in 1861. As a senator in Washington, he faced antisemitic charges, even though he was not a practicing Jew and had married a Christian woman.

Union forces imprisoned Yulee at the end of the war. He was held longer in confinement than any other Southern leader except Confederate President Jefferson Davis. After his release, Yulee returned to Florida and helped build a statewide railroad before returning to live in Washington in 1880. He is buried in Georgetown's Oak Hill Cemetery.

NEITHER BLUE NOR GRAY

Courtesy of West Point Museum Art Collection, United States Military Academy

AN OFFICER'S DILEMMA (1804-1887)

In 1846, West Point graduate Major Alfred Mordecai became commander of the Washington Arsenal, now Fort McNair. Mordecai also served as assistant to the Secretary of War and to the Chief of Ordnance.

In 1861, Mordecai sought an army post in California to avoid fighting in the Civil War. When the request was denied, he resigned his commission rather than serve against his native North Carolina. After refusing an offer to serve in the Confederacy, Mordecai ended his military career.

MEN WITH THE PRESIDENT'S EAR

Isachar Zacharie

Courtesy of Robert Marcus

Executive Mansion,
Washington, Sep. 19, 1864.
Dr. Zacharie
Dear Sir
I thank you again for the deep interest you have constantly taken in the Union cause. The personal matter on behalf of your friend, which you mention, shall be fully and fairly considered when presented.
Yours truly
A. Lincoln

Courtest of Library of Congress

Letter from President Lincoln to Isachar Zacharie, 1864, thanking Zacharie for "the deep interest you have constantly taken in the Union cause."

LINCOLN'S FOOT DOCTOR (1827-1900)

Isachar Zacharie, a successful New York chiropodist, moved to Washington, where his practice included Union generals, Cabinet secretaries, and the President.

In 1863, at Lincoln's request, Zacharie met with Judah Benjamin, the Jewish Secretary of State of the Confederacy, to propose peace negotiations. Opposed by Lincoln's cabinet, the plan was quickly dropped. Many of Lincoln's advisors did not trust Dr. Zacharie and derided him as doing little more than cutting toenails and removing corns. Zacharie later campaigned for Lincoln's reelection among Jews in the North.

"ZACHARIE ENJOYED MR. LINCOLN'S CONFIDENCE, PERHAPS MORE THAN ANY OTHER PRIVATE INDIVIDUAL . . . [AND WAS] PERHAPS THE MOST FAVORED FAMILY VISITOR TO THE WHITE HOUSE."

- *New York World*, 1864

Simon Wolf

JHSGW Collections, gift of Bernard Nordlinger

SPOKESMAN FOR THE JEWISH COMMUNITY (1836-1923)

In 1862, lawyer Simon Wolf left Cleveland for Washington. An active member of both Washington Hebrew Congregation and B'nai B'rith, Wolf was an eloquent orator and influential leader. He formed close relationships with every U.S. president from Abraham Lincoln to Woodrow Wilson.

A WHITE HOUSE VISIT

Early in the war, Wolf learned that a Jewish soldier was to be executed the next morning for having deserted his unit to travel to his mother's deathbed. Wolf went to Lincoln at 2 a.m. to plead for the soldier's life. He said, "If your dying mother had summoned you to her bedside to receive her last message...would you have been a deserter to her who gave you birth, rather than deserter in law but not in fact to the flag to which you had sworn allegiance?"

Lincoln pardoned the soldier, and his secretary, John Hay, immediately telegraphed the stay of execution.

"My primary purpose has been to prove that the Jewish people . . . have been unfailing in their devotion to their country's cause."

-Simon Wolf,
The American Jew as Patriot, Soldier, and Citizen

"Mr. Wolf, you have done your duty and I know that you are a loyal citizen."

-Secretary of War Edwin Stanton (as quoted in *Presidents I Have Known*)

ARRESTED FOR DEFENDING OTHERS

During the war, Wolf was detained for serving as attorney for Southern Jews charged with espionage and for his membership in B'nai B'rith. Accusing Wolf of being a traitor, Colonel Lafayette C. Baker of the War Department threatened him with imprisonment and called B'nai B'rith "a disloyal organization, which…is helping the traitors."

When Secretary of War Edwin Stanton learned of the situation, he called it an outrage and promptly had Wolf released.

SETTING THE RECORD STRAIGHT

In 1895, in response to charges that Jews had evaded military service, Wolf published a comprehensive review of Jewish service in the American military. *The American Jew as Patriot, Soldier and Citizen* lists more than 8,000 Jewish soldiers who fought in the Civil War. Wolf concluded that "the enlistment of Jewish soldiers, north and south, reached proportions considerably in excess of their ratio to the general population."

AFTER THE WAR: AN ELDER STATESMAN

After the war, Wolf held numerous local and national leadership positions.

President Ulysses S. Grant named him Recorder of Deeds, making him one of the first Jews to hold public office in Washington. He also served as president of Washington Hebrew Congregation in the 1870s. In 1881, President Garfield appointed him Consul General to Egypt.

As chairman of the Board of Delegates of Civil and Religious Rights (previously called the Board of Delegates of American Israelites) and president of the International Order of B'nai B'rith, Wolf was an outspoken advocate on national and international Jewish issues. In 1869, he appealed to President Grant urging the United States to protest the expulsion of thousands of Russian Jews from their homes. In 1903, he helped organize a national petition protesting the Russian government's actions in the Kishinev massacre.

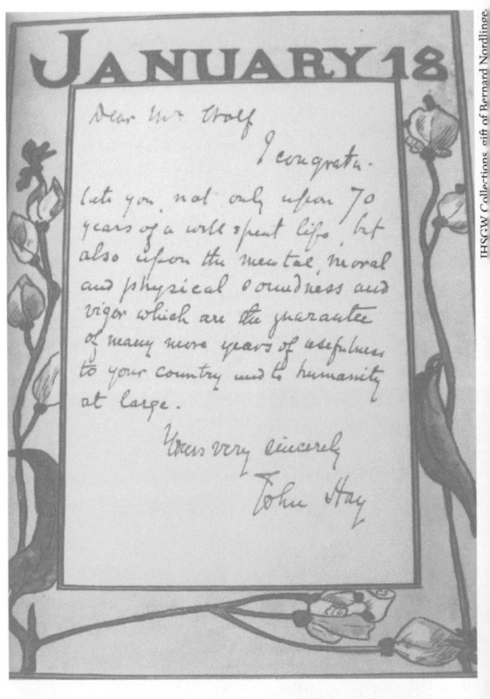

JANUARY 18

Dear Mr Wolf

I congratulate you not only upon 70 years of a well spent life, but also upon the mental, moral and physical soundness and vigor which are the guarantee of many more years of usefulness to your country and to humanity at large.

Yours very sincerely

John Hay

JHSGW Collections, gift of Bernard Nordlinge

Secretary of State John Hay, Lincoln's private secretary during the Civil War, wrote this note congratulating Wolf on his 70th birthday in 1905.

Adolphus Solomons

Courtesy of B'nai B'rith Klutznick National Jewish Museum

LOCAL AND NATIONAL LEADER (1826-1910)

With Franklin Philp, Adolphus Solomons ran a successful bookstore at 332 Pennsylvania Avenue, NW. Widely respected by both President Lincoln and the Jewish community, he frequently served as a link between them.

After the Civil War, Solomons served in the Washington, D.C. House of Delegates and on the Presidential Inauguration Committee for Ulysses S. Grant. In 1881, Solomons helped Clara Barton found the American Red Cross. He was instrumental in the building of Adas Israel's synagogue in 1876.

BATTLEFIELD RABBIS

When the Volunteer Act of 1861 mandated that only Christians could be military chaplains, the Board of Delegates of American Israelites sent Rabbi Arnold Fischel to Washington to lobby for change. Using Solomons's bookstore as his headquarters, Fischel succeeded when Lincoln signed a law on July 17, 1862, for the first time permitting rabbis to become chaplains.

Courtesy of Robert Marcus

Army Navy atlas published by Philp & Solomons, stationers for Congress and the armed forces, in 1863.

"We passed a pleasant Sabbath with Mr. Adolphus Solomons whose place of business [on] Pennsylvania Avenue is the resort of men of letters... We were pleased to find Mr. S. doing so well in the capital, especially as he is one of the very few Israelites there who observe the Sabbath."

- *The Jewish Messenger*, January 24, 1862

JHSGW Collections

Philp & Solomons served as publishers for famed Civil War photographer Alexander Gardner, whose Metropolitan Gallery was located upstairs at 332 Pennsylvania Avenue, NW.

LINCOLN AND THE JEWS

Harold Holzer

Abraham Lincoln – America's "Great Emancipator" – never liberated any Jewish people. But in death, America's Jews compared him reverentially to Moses. Like the prophet and lawgiver from Exodus, Lincoln had led people from bondage, yet did not live to see the Promised Land. As Rabbi M. R. Deleeuw put it in his eulogy at Congregation B'nai Israel in New York on April 19, 1865, Lincoln "had brought this nation within reach of the great boon he sought to attain," but "was not destined to taste the sweets of the peace he had so zealously labored to establish." The analogy was not lost on the nation's small but vocal Jewish community. On a more practical level, Lincoln had not only befriended Jewish people throughout his life but made several major presidential decisions that benefited American Jewry.

This is not to suggest that American Jews had an easy time during the Civil War era. They were a tiny and often oppressed minority of the population: 150,000 out of about 32 million – just half of one percent – although the country did boast vibrant centers of Jewish life in New York, Boston, Philadelphia, and New Orleans. Some 6,000 Jews served in the

: Alexandar Gardner
:ograph, one of the last taken
braham Lincoln, appeared
card printed by the firm of
p & Solomons, 1865.

American military, a number that included twelve generals, many surgeons, and six Medal of Honor winners.

But it was not a monolithic group: Northern Jews remained loyal to the Union, Southern Jews mainly to the Confederacy and to slavery. In fact, Southern society may have in some ways been more hospitable to Jews than that of the North. In an era in which Jews filled no major roles in the Lincoln administration, Judah P. Benjamin became Secretary of State of the Confederacy. Yet Benjamin's elevation did not eliminate bigotry there. According to one Southern diarist in 1861:

> The Jews are at work. Having no nationality, all wars are harvests for them. It has been so from the day of their dispersion. Now they are scouring the country in all directions, buying all the goods they can find in distant cities, and even from the country stores. These they will keep, until the prices of consumption shall raise a greedy demand for all descriptions of merchandise.

Perhaps it should come as no surprise that in this atmosphere, one county in Georgia was actually consumed by an uprising aimed at driving out Jews.

Things could be just as dangerous, however, in the supposedly enlightened North. In New York, the same city where the "Jews' Hospital" changed its longtime admissions policy so it could treat wounded soldiers of all faiths (today the once-modest institution is known as Mount Sinai Medical Center), draft rioters attacked and pillaged Jewish stores just a few days after the Battle of Gettysburg. When the Union Treasury began issuing paper money, one Confederate newspaper taunted, "Why are Lincoln's green-backs like the Jews? Because they come from Abraham and have no redeemer." Against that backdrop of discrimination stood a *modern* Abraham: Abraham Lincoln.

A New York rabbi named Morris Raphall came to the White House early in the war to ask Lincoln to promote his son to the rank of lieutenant in the Union Army. Lincoln had declared that day a national prayer and fast day, and after he listened to the rabbi's plea, he asked, "As God's minister, is it not your duty to be home today to pray with your people for the success of our armies, as is being done in every loyal church throughout the North?"

Taken aback, the rabbi managed to explain that his assistant was doing so in his place. "Ah," Lincoln replied, "That is different." Then he wrote out the promotion, handed it to Raphall, and said, "Now, doctor, you can go home and do your *own* praying."

Raphall was not the first Jew Lincoln ever encountered, but it is fair to say that Lincoln probably never saw one until he was about 30 years old, when he first met a fellow Illinois lawyer named Abraham Jonas. Jonas became an enthusiastic political supporter, whom Lincoln would call one of his "most valued friends." He later appointed Jonas a postmaster, a position he held until his death, when Lincoln quietly transferred the plum job to his widow (at a time when he was reluctant to name his own female relatives to such coveted patronage posts). Lincoln even paroled Jonas's son, a captured Rebel, to visit his father on his deathbed. The sins of the son were not visited on the loyal father.

Lincoln counted other Jews among his friends and allies: Julius Hammerslough, one of his hometown Springfield merchants, who attended his inauguration and later helped raise funds to build his tomb; and Henry Rice, a clothing retailer who sold Lincoln "duds," as his famous customer referred to them, on the Illinois prairie. Photographer Samuel Alschuler lent Lincoln a velvet-trimmed coat to wear in a photograph taken in Urbana, Illinois, in 1858. Two years later, and now relocated to Chicago, Alschuler took another portrait of Lincoln, now President-elect. It turned out to be the first ever made of him with a beard.

Bavarian-born Chicago merchant Abraham Kohn, president of Congregation Anshe Maariv (Men of the West), was another staunch Republican supporter. Just before Lincoln left Illinois for the White House, Kohn sent the president-elect a flag emblazoned with Hebrew writing from Deuteronomy 31: "Be strong and of good courage; be not afraid neither be thou dismayed for the Lord thy God is with thee whithersoever thou goest."

A few days later, as Lincoln left his Springfield home for Washington, he gave a farewell speech to his neighbors offering words clearly inspired by Kohn. That day, Lincoln declared his trust in a God who can "go with me, and remain with you, and be everywhere for good." Here was an Old Testament inspiration, direct from a Jewish friend. Later witnesses remembered seeing Kohn's flag on display at the White House.

But the most fascinating – and influential – of Lincoln's Jewish acquaintances was undoubtedly his Jewish chiropodist, Isachar Zacharie. A New York newspaper described him as having "a splendid Roman nose, fashionable whiskers, an eloquent tongue, a dazzling diamond breastpin," and, most important of all for treating a patient with chronically aching feet, "great skill in his profession."

In 1862, Lincoln heard that Zacharie could boast in his résumé of having had feet of Clay – *Henry* Clay, that is, Lincoln's personal and political hero. So the President sent for him to see if the chiropodist could alleviate his aching corns. One newspaper joked, "It would seem . . . that all of our past troubles have originated not so much with the head [of the nation] but with the feet of the nation. Dr. Zacharie has shown us precisely where the shoe pinches."

Jokes aside, Zacharie worked wonders with Lincoln. As the President put it, in an endorsement of his skill, "Dr. Zacharie has operated on my feet with great success and considerable addition to my comfort." Not everyone who met the chiropodist was able to overcome prejudice. One general assessed Zacharie "the lowest and vulgarest form of Jew Peddlars," adding, "It is enough to condemn Mr. Lincoln that he can make a friend of such an odious creature."

Lincoln was not swayed by such prejudice. He not only retained Zacharie as his physician, bit he also found other ways for him to serve the Union as an unofficial envoy to Jewish communities in the South with an eye toward rebuilding their ties to the Union. The doctor turned up in New Orleans, for example, supposedly to arrange financial aid for that city to ease it back under federal authority. Later, Lincoln twice sent him to Richmond on mysterious missions. In return, Zacharie peppered Lincoln with boastful letters and gifts like fresh pineapples, bananas, and hominy grits.

Zacharie worked hard for Lincoln's re-election in 1864, writing to assure the President during the campaign:

> The Isrelites [sic] with but few exceptions they will vote for you. I understand them well.... I have secured good and trustworthy men to attend to them on Election day. My men have been all the week seeing that their masses are proparly [sic] registered—so that all will be right.

Zacharie's efforts predictably aroused a stir among – who else? – his fellow Jews, some of whom took issue with Zacharie's claim that he could "deliver" the Jewish vote as a bloc. "There is no 'Jewish vote,'" the editor of the *Jewish Messenger*, Meyer Isaacs, wrote angrily to Lincoln, "and if there were it could not be bought." The fracas threatened to erupt into a political crisis until Lincoln ordered an aide to write a letter assuring Jewish leaders that no one had ever pledged the Jewish vote to the President, and he in turn had offered no inducements to secure it.

The fact that Lincoln utilized a character like Zacharie remains surprising. The doctor was rather full of himself. In 1863 he talked about "the great responsibility resting upon me," words Lincoln had more appropriately employed to describe the burdens on *him!* A week before Election Day 1864, Zacharie bragged that he had accomplished "one of the Largest things that has been done in the campaign." Then he complained to the exhausted President that *he* was tired. "I wish to God all was over," he wrote, "for I am used up, but 3 years ago, I promised I would elect you, and if you are not it shall not be my fault." Notwithstanding such boasting, Lincoln saw something in his doctor that historians have never quite understood. Lincoln *was* an excellent judge of character, so it's difficult not to conclude that somehow, Zacharie did serve him beneficially – and not just medically.

Critics point to an odd memorandum Lincoln wrote during the war that began, "About Jews," and went on to offer instructions on seemingly unrelated matters: issuing to "Dr. Zacharie a pass to go to Savannah," and providing some kind of hearing to a Mr. "Blumberg, at Baltimore." In a way, the memo suggests that Lincoln tended to think of Jews as a nation within the nation, perhaps not as truly assimilated as American Jews thought themselves to be. On the other hand, the memo also sent a signal to the bureaucracy that the President believed that Jews, at least these particular Jews, should be treated decently by the government.

There were two real tests of Lincoln's tolerance during the Civil War. A year into the war, there was still not one Jewish chaplain in the armed services. Federal law required that all chaplains be "regularly ordained ministers of some Christian denomination."

Jews wanted their own. They had a champion in Ohio Congressman Clement L. Valandigham, who took to the House floor to demand equal chaplaincy rights for Jews. Unfortunately, they could not have recruited a more counterproductive ally. Valandigham was a so-called "Copperhead," an anti-war Democrat. "Valiant Val" later would be arrested for treason and expelled from the Union. His support guaranteed defeat for expanding chaplaincy rights.

The issue might have died there had it not been for the so-called "Allen incident." Michael Allen was a rabbinical student elected chaplain of a largely Jewish regiment headed by a Colonel Max Freedman. When the army found out about him, they pressured him into quitting, arguing that he was not yet fully ordained. Colonel Freedman promptly named a fully ordained New York rabbi named Arnold Fischel to take his place. But the U. S. Sanitary Commission, the charity that attended to the soldiers' medical and moral needs, turned him down, too, citing the law that required all chaplains to be Christians.

Frustrated, Jewish leaders went public. They wrote editorials for Jewish periodicals, got liberal newspapers to support them, and finally sent a delegation to the White House. There, Dr. Fischel begged Lincoln to recognize "the principle of religious liberty . . . the constitutional rights of the Jewish community, and the welfare of Jewish volunteers" who were dying in battle without access to spiritual support.

Lincoln swiftly pledged, "I shall try to have a new law broad enough to cover what is desired by you in behalf of the Israelites." The following summer, the law was duly amended to include all "regularly ordained ministers of *some* denomination." The word "Christian" was expunged. That September, Lincoln named Rabbi Jacob Frankel of Philadelphia the first Jewish chaplain in American military history. The Jews, under Lincoln, had reversed four score years of institutionalized discrimination within the army.

Another crisis followed, a result of an action by one of the war's greatest heroes, Ulysses S. Grant. After his triumph at the Battle of Shiloh, the general inexplicably began imagining Jews infiltrating his encampments en masse, speculating, profiteering, and conducting other wicked business unchecked. Grant was determined to root them out. In July 1862, he ordered his commanders to inspect all visitors' baggage and confiscate contraband, noting, "Jews should receive special attention." That November he advised another officer, "Refuse all permits ... the Isrealites [sic] especially should be kept out." A day later he repeated, "No Jews are to be permitted to travel on the Rail Road southward from any point. They are such an intolerable nuisance, that the department must be purged of them." Weeks afterward, he was still railing about "the total disregard and evasion of orders by the Jews," admitting, "my policy is to exclude them as far as practicable." A camp newspaper not surprisingly echoed the popular general: The Jews were "sharks, feeding upon the soldiers."

Then, Grant's own father turned up in camp, hand-in-hand with some Jewish cotton brokers eager for profit, though no greedier for money than the elder Mr. Grant. Perhaps believing his father had been duped, the general let his hostility run wild. On December 17, 1862, he issued his infamous General Orders No. 11, declaring in part:

> The Jews, as a class violating every regulation of trade ... are hereby expelled from the department within 24 hours. ... Post commanders will see that all of this class of people be ... required to leave, and any one returning after such notification will be arrested and held in confinement.

Reaction was swift. A Jewish captain named Philip Trounstine promptly resigned his commission, complaining of "taunts and malice." Respected Northern rabbis unleashed a firestorm of criticism from the pulpit and in the press. Even Grant's greatest Washington champion, Illinois Congressman Elihu Washburne, admitted, "Your order touching the Jews has kicked up quite a dust among the Israelites. They came here in crowds. ..."

Some of the crowds went directly to the President, who might easily have ignored the outcry for fear of humiliating one of his most valuable military assets. To Lincoln's credit, he did not excuse or cover up. He came to the rescue. When a delegation led by Cesar Kaskel visited him to lodge a formal protest, the President supposedly said, "So the children of Israel were forced out of the happy land of Canaan?"

A clever delegate shot back, "Yes, and that is why we have come unto Father Abraham's bosom asking protection." Replied Lincoln, "That protection you shall have." Another group headed by Rabbi Isaac Mayer Wise soon followed, and Lincoln told them, "I don't like to see a class or nationality condemned on account of a few sinners." Wise remembered, "The President fully convinced us that he knew of no distinction between Jews and Gentiles and that he feels none against any nationality and especially against Israelites."

In one of the rare occasions in which he ever overruled his prize general, Abraham Lincoln made sure that General Orders No. 11 was rescinded a few weeks after its publication. He did not mind expelling peddlers, Lincoln explained privately. But, as he put it, Grant had "proscribed a whole class, some of whom are fighting in our ranks." This was unacceptable. Another threat to the legal standing of Jewish citizens had been recognized and corrected. Whether it inspired Jews to vote as a bloc for Lincoln's re-election the following fall remains impossible to know, but the positive impact on Lincoln's reputation was incontestable.

History books note the irony of the fact that like Jesus, Lincoln was slain on Good Friday. It is seldom observed that the 1865 calamity also occurred during Passover weekend. Seders that season were dedicated in part to Lincoln's memory.

Synagogues across the North draped themselves in black and devoted Sabbath and holiday sermons, as one Jewish newspaper reported, "to the grief that sorrowed the hearts of the people." Jews took an active part in the Lincoln funeral in Washington. At the public ceremonies in New York, a rabbi was even asked to recite a prayer. One young local Jewish shopkeeper named Abraham Abraham was so moved that he bought a bust of Lincoln, draped it in black, and displayed it in his window. The shop later became the department store of Abraham & Strauss. In Chicago, a special canopy was provided by the city's Jews, inscribed with the Hebrew lament: "The beauty of Israel is slain upon the high places."

Rabbi Isaac Mayer Wise, who had earlier called Lincoln a "primitive," now praised "the spirit and principles of the man." At Congregation Shearith Israel in Manhattan the mourners' Kaddish was recited for the first time in memory of a non-Jew, inspiring a protest from some outraged Orthodox Jews but praise from most congregants. If Lincoln could break precedent by opening up the army to Jewish chaplaincy, then synagogues could say Kaddish for their gentile champion. Even in the South, Jewish leaders acknowledged a special bond between Lincoln and the Jews and a special sorrow at his loss. It was attributable mainly to Lincoln's acts of compassion and justice, but perhaps, also, to the fact that his religious beliefs seemed so universal.

Lincoln had once summed up his faith: "When I do good I feel good, and when I do bad I feel bad, and that's my religion." Perhaps it is no accident that the sentiment is remarkably close to what Hillel urged in his teachings: "To forbear doing unto others what would displease *us*."

That deceptively simple but poignant philosophy made Lincoln seem to Jews of his day like God's child and America's father at one and the same time. When Lincoln died, many Jews really did feel "the beauty of Israel was slain upon the high places." But as Rabbi Samuel Adler put it at Temple Emanu-el in New York City on April 19, 1865: "Abraham Lincoln has not fallen. He is lost to us but he is as Light ... and remains with us in memory and adoration and will so remain for ever." Rabbi Adler called him "Father Abraham" that day, a rare tribute from the pulpit echoed at synagogues throughout the nation during that Passover of mourning. "Fear not, Abraham," Rabbi Samuel Meyer Isaacs declared, quoting the Bible, from the pulpit of the Broadway synagogue, "I am thy shield; thy reward shall be exceedingly great."

History has vindicated that prediction.

Sources

Breslaw, Elaine Meir, "Jewish Chaplains in a Christian Army," *Columbiad*, 1 (Summer 1977): 86-92.

Bunker, Gary L. and John Appel, "'Shoddy,' Anti-Semitism and the Civil War," *American Jewish History*, 5 (1994): 43-71.

Hamilton, Charles and Lloyd Ostendorf, *Lincoln in Photographs: An Album of Every Known Pose.* Norman, Oklahoma: University of Oklahoma Press, 1963.

Hertz, Emanuel, ed. *Abraham Lincoln: The Tribute of the Synagogue.* New York: Bloch Publishing, 1927.

Korn, Bertram W. *American Jewry and the Civil War.* Philadelphia: The Jewish Publication Society of America, 1951.

Markens, Isaac. *Abraham Lincoln and the Jews.* New York: Privately Printed, 1909.

Pool, David De Sola, "The Diary of Chaplain Michael M. Allen, September 1861," *American Jewish Historical Society Journal*, 39 (1948).

Rosen, Robert N. *The Jewish Confederates.* Columbia, SC: University of South Carolina Press, 2000.

Rubinger, Naphtali J. *Abraham Lincoln and the Jews.* New York: Jonathan David, 1962.

Wolf, William J. *The Almost Chosen People: A Study of the Religion of Abraham Lincoln.* Garden City, NY: Doubleday, 1959.

Virginian Jews in the Civil War

Dr. Melvin I. Urofsky

Virginia Jews differed little from their neighbors regarding the desirability of secession in the winter of 1860-61 but once the decision had been reached, they too rallied to the cause. Men flocked to the Stars and Bars, and the two leading Richmond militia groups both had significant Jewish membership. In Petersburg, Norfolk, and elsewhere, the story was the same: whether they owned slaves or not, nearly all Virginia Jews supported the decision to secede, and the men joined the army to defend that decision. Myer Angle, the first president of Congregation Beth Ahabah in Richmond, watched all six of his sons go off to fight for the Confederacy. Many Jews gave their lives, and Richmond set apart a special Soldiers' Section in the Hebrew Cemetery containing 31 graves of both Richmond and non-Richmond men. Until after World War II, it was the only Jewish military cemetery in the world.

Just before the war, Henry Gintzberger arrived in Salem, Virginia. An itinerant peddler in his mid-twenties, he may have been the first Jew ever seen in that small community, and his

ew of Union-occupied
exandria, Virginia, 1864.

arrival became a legend in town. Soon after his appearance in Salem, he fell sick with a high fever. The local townspeople would not allow a stranger to go unattended, and a resident took Gintzberger into his house, where the family nursed him through a long illness. By the time he recovered, the war had broken out. Perhaps to show his gratitude to the people of Salem, Gintzberger enlisted with the other men of the town in the Salem Flying Artillery. He served with the unit until killed in action at Cold Harbor in 1864.

The great sculptor Sir Moses Ezekiel remembered all his life his experiences as a cadet at the Virginia Military Institute, when he and his unit participated in the battle of New Market. "Ten of our boys were killed in the battle of Newmarket," he recalled. "It was later one of the most sacred duties in my life to remodel my bronze statue of *Virginia Mourning Her Dead* to be placed on the parade ground of the V.M.I., overlooking the graves of my dead comrades, so that their memory may go on in imperishable bronze, sounding their heroism and Virginia's memory down through all ages and forever."

If Ezekiel remembered the gallantry and pageantry, others recalled great anguish. Isaac Hirsch of Fredericksburg joined Company A of Virginia's 30th Infantry Regiment in May 1861, and he kept a diary of his wartime experiences. He saw action at minor skirmishes at Aquia and Manassas, but after a particularly bloody fight near Warrenton, he wrote, "I left the field (of blackened bodies) with a heavy heart, as I had never seen the Romance of War in this shape before. ... I got back to camp a wiser man than I had left it." After he mustered out in the fall of 1863, his last entry read, "Got home last night. Thank God. Home once more."

Families throughout Virginia and the South often faced internal tensions about secession. Jacob A. Levy had two sons who fought for their state: Captain E. J. Levy of the Richmond Blues and Private Isaac J. Levy, who fell in battle near Petersburg in 1864. Two of Levy's nephews, however, Abraham I. Levy and Jacob E. Hyneman, chose to serve in the Union army. Jacob Ezekiel, despite his son's passion for the war, remained a staunch Unionist, but because both his sons had enlisted in the Confederate Army, he could not leave Richmond. He remained in business, doing what he could to help Yankees captured and incarcerated in Libby Prison. In Charlottesville, Isaac Leterman fought for the Union and his younger brother Simon for the rebellion, while Simon's wife, Hannah, served as a Confederate nurse.

Jews made up a significant portion of some units, and on two occasions Robert E. Lee had to refuse High Holiday furloughs for Jewish troops on the grounds that their absence would greatly weaken his forces. On at least one occasion, the request came from Maximilian Michelbacher, who, according to several sources, served in all but name as chaplain to Jewish soldiers in the Confederate army. Michelbacher also pleaded with Lee to commute the sentence of a young Jewish soldier, Private Isaac Arnold of the 8th Alabama Regiment, whom a court-martial had found guilty of cowardice under fire and sentenced to death. Michelbacher did not question the integrity of the court but asked that justice be tempered with mercy. On this occasion, he succeeded, at least in regard to the unfortunate Arnold. However, Michelbacher could not persuade Lee to allow Jewish troops furlough for Passover. As the general noted, "I think it more than probable that the army will be engaged in active operations, when, of course, no one would wish to be absent from its ranks."

Lee apparently tried to help on such requests whenever he could. When a Richmond soldier asked leave to attend services at the synagogue, his captain refused and marked on the letter: "Disapproved. If such applications were granted, the whole army would turn Jews or shaking Quakers." When the papers came to Lee's desk, however, he granted the request and returned it to the captain "with the advice that he should always respect the religious views and feelings of others."

Because so much fighting took place in Virginia, women often knew that their husbands or sons were encamped in the vicinity and would visit them, or at least try to do so. Years after the war, Rosena Levy recalled going to the camps, getting permission from the officers, worrying when she learned her husband had been captured, and then, after he had been exchanged and quite ill, bringing him home to nurse. Mary Gerst, on the other hand, declined her husband's suggestion that she come to see him at his camp in Ashland, declaring that "I do not think a military camp is any place for ladies."

Women did much of the nursing during the war. Jewish women did not minister only to wounded Jewish soldiers nor did Christian women only take care of their own. Major Alexander

Hart of Louisiana suffered a severe leg wound. The surgeon, believing recovery was impossible, wanted to amputate the limb immediately. But the woman to whose house he had been carried begged the doctor to hold off for a few days, saying she would tend to the patient herself. So young and handsome a man, she declared, should not lose a leg. The doctor reluctantly agreed. When he returned a few days later he discovered that the leg had started to heal, and eventually Hart regained full health. After the war, Hart always tried to see his benefactress whenever he came to Richmond.

This act of selfless kindness by a Christian woman to a young Jewish soldier seems a far more accurate reflection of what most Virginians felt toward their Jewish neighbors than the mindless diatribes of a handful of bigots.

Nevertheless, in both the North and South, the war triggered antisemitic sentiments that had been, for the most part, relatively absent before 1861. Economic tensions, personal fears and frustrations, and the mass passions generated by war required an outlet, however, and in the past the victims of these conditions often had been Jews. Given the ferocity of the war, the manifestations were comparatively mild – there were no pogroms on either side – and, perhaps more important, not only did Jews openly oppose the prejudice, but non-Jews also came to their defense.

Charles Francis Adams noted in his diary a conversation he had had on the eve of the war in which Senator Andrew Johnson of Tennessee ranted against Jews: "There's that [David] Yulee, miserable little cuss! I remember him in the House – the contemptible little Jew – standing there and begging us – yes!

begging us to let Florida in as a state ... and now that despicable little beggar stands up in the Senate and talks about *her* rights." After finishing with Yulee, Johnson started in on Judah P. Benjamin: "There's another Jew – that miserable Benjamin! He looks on a country and a government as he would on a suit of old clothes. He sold out the old one; and he would sell out the new if he could in so doing make two or three millions." The prominence of Yulee and Benjamin in Rebel ranks led some Northerners to assert that all Jews were secessionists and that there would never have been a rebellion had Jewish bankers not planned it in order to enhance their profits.

There were instances of antisemitism in the Confederacy as well. Senator Henry S. Foote of Tennessee proposed to amend that state's constitution to ban Jews from coming within twelve miles of the capital. Such expressions, however, were rare. The Confederate Congress did not exclude non-Christians when establishing chaplaincies, and no Southern general attempted to exile Jews from areas under his command. In Virginia, invitations went to rabbis as well as to Christian ministers to offer prayers at the beginning of the legislative day, and when some groups tried to secure special privileges for Christians, the efforts always failed under a barrage of criticism invoking the names of Jefferson and Madison.

Antisemitism did exist, some of it, ironically, sparked by the same Judah P. Benjamin who so angered Andrew Johnson. Benjamin had been born in the Virgin Islands of British parents who later moved to Charleston, South Carolina. Although he never converted or denied his Jewish birth, Benjamin took no interest in Jewish affairs; nonetheless, he was identified by both friend and foe as a Jew. Elected to the United States Senate in 1852, Benjamin sided with the secessionists and served in the Confederate cabinet as attorney general, secretary of war, and secretary of state. After the war, he moved to England rather than live in the defeated South, and there he became a distinguished barrister.

Whereas Northerners attacked Benjamin as a secessionist, Southern antisemites tended to blame him for all the ills of the Confederacy. A letter to the editor of the *Richmond Enquirer* believed it blasphemous for a Jew to hold so high an office and maintained that Southern prayers would be better received by the Almighty if Benjamin were ousted from the cabinet. President Jefferson Davis once found himself assailed in violent language by a Virginian for appointing a Jew to his cabinet. Davis steadfastly opposed this and all other attempts to get rid of Benjamin, whose abilities he recognized and valued and whom he counted as a friend.

Many Southerners even charged Benjamin and other Jews with profiteering. The Union blockade of southern ports led to severe shortages, and many people engaged in smuggling and profiteering. Although blockade running has often been depicted as a romantic high adventure, in fact it was dangerous and far from glamorous. Philip Whitlock, a tailor in private life and quartermaster clerk with the Richmond Grays who had been present at the hanging of John Brown recounted in his diary how he and his brother-in-law, Ellis Abram, ran the blockade along with four colleagues. They had no trouble getting to the Potomac, where they found a black man willing to row them over. Moving with muffled oars, they spotted a Union gunboat when they were halfway there. The hired oarsman wanted to turn back, but one of the passengers convinced him to continue by putting a revolver to his head. Whitlock and Abram made their way to New York, where they stayed for nearly a week buying fine-toothed combs, tobacco pipes, pins, needles, pencils, and other small goods that would fit in their hand luggage and then headed home.

This proved an even more arduous journey than they had expected. The two hid in a tobacco barn in Maryland for nearly two weeks before they could cross over to Virginia where they were arrested by a Confederate captain. After their release, they discovered that about half their purchases had disappeared. By the time they got back to Richmond and sold the other half, they had just about broken even.

Whitlock's blockade-running escapade was a minor event, and from all evidence, Jews played a relatively small role in smuggling. But the high prices for such contraband led to widespread anger among the populace. This anger led at times to efforts to make Jews the scapegoats. During the 1863 bread riots in Richmond, agitators charged that Jewish speculators had caused the shortages and were lining their own pockets at the expense of true patriots. In a sermon preached in Fredericksburg on a Confederate fast day (May 27, 1863), Michelbacher rebutted the accusations and declared flatly that "the Israelites are not speculators nor extortioners." The sermon was widely reprinted in both the North and the South.

The *Richmond Examiner* often charged that Jews had no loyalty to the Confederacy and merely wanted to make money out of the war, primarily by providing inferior goods to the army. A cartoon, "Shoddy or the Vulture of the Camp," was popular north and south of the Mason-Dixon line, and the *Examiner* asserted that Jews "flocked as vultures to every point of gain." Allegations by the *Examiner* led the U.S. House of Representatives to appoint a special committee in early 1864 to look into the charges. They were found totally baseless.

Although Union troops had tried to capture Richmond almost from the beginning of the war, the city withstood conquest until the end. Other sections of the state proved less fortunate. Parts of the Shenandoah Valley and much of northern Virginia were occupied by federal troops through most of the war. In early 1862, Northern forces under the command of Marcus M. Spiegel, a German immigrant who had settled in Ohio, occupied Woodstock. In a letter to his wife, he wrote of surprising Jews he met in towns under his jurisdiction. When he recognized a Jew, he would use a few words of Hebrew or Yiddish and then smile at their reaction. They would ask in return if he was Jewish, and upon receiving a firm yes, they would invite him and his officers to their home for dinner and do all they could to treat him with respect.

Although Jews had not lived in Alexandria as long as they had in Richmond or Norfolk, many of the Jewish families there had strong Southern sentiments, and several of the young men served with the Confederate army. On the day that Virginia voted to secede from the Union, Henry Schwarz ran an advertisement in the *Alexandria Gazette.* Despite its efforts at lightheartedness, there was an underlying tone of despair that affected many of the city's residents:

> The War has certainly begun.
> Go to SCHWARZ's you'll see there is no fun;
> He'll sell you for 25 cents the 'Panic Envelope',
> Containing Hose, Handkerchiefs, Mitts, Combs, and Soap.
> In others are Pocket Books, Cravats, Collars and Sleeves,
> And everything that mortal can conceive;
> The motto of selling so cheap,
> Is simply as he needs money a heap
> As there is trouble all over the land,
> He is anxious to dispose of Goods on hand;
> Call and see him or send in your order,
> And get the 'Panic Envelope' for only a quarter.
> As for the worth of your money, you need not be mistaken.
> It is as sure as Fort Sumter is taken.

Only a few weeks later, the New York Zouaves marched into Alexandria and occupied the city for the duration of the war. Those who remained found themselves subject to the indignities of occupation, and in 1863, Union officials drew up a list of Alexandria citizens, including several Jews, who were considered disloyal. They received an alternative of either proving their loyalty at once or facing deportation behind Southern lines.

The provost marshal's records described Joseph Rosenthal and his brother Albert, who owned a shoe store on King Street, as having been "formerly connected with all rebel movements while rebs were here." The report also labeled Simon Waterman, who had lived in Virginia for at least fifteen years, as "Secesh but guarded in conversation." Waterman's wife, Caroline, also found her name on the list. The Rosenthals managed to prove their loyalty, but the Watermans could not, and only a last-minute rescission of the deportation order by the secretary of war prevented their exile. Jews, however, were treated equally with their neighbors. In fact, the military-controlled city council named Peter Seldner to the wartime board of health in 1863, perhaps the first Alexandria Jew to hold public office.

Richmond escaped outright occupation during most of the war, but in April 1865, Lee's defense line at Petersburg collapsed, and he sent a message to Davis to evacuate Richmond. Many citizens fled. The majority of the Jews, who had clearly supported the Confederate cause, decided to remain and take their chances during the occupation.

On April 2, the day before Union troops entered the city, Confederate officials set fire to the large stores of tobacco that had accumulated in the city to prevent their falling into enemy hands. A strong wind blew up from the south, and before long, much of the downtown business district had been turned into an inferno. In her diary, Emma Mordecai recalled seeing the glow of the flames, hearing one explosion after another, and feeling concern for relatives and friends still in the city. Soon after, concern turned to fear as she and her sister-in-law had to deal with marauding troops and freed slaves and then the certainty of knowing that her beloved Richmond had been destroyed.

As the 4th Massachusetts Cavalry rode down Main Street, the men were greeted with scowls and jeers from the bystanders, but as they approached one house, a second-floor window opened, and a handsome young woman flung to the breeze a large flag showing the Stars and Stripes. Major Atherton H. Stevens and his men wheeled in front of the house and "gave a lusty cheer for Old Glory and another for the fair woman who had gladdened their hearts." Had they known the truth of this deception, they might not have cheered so lustily.

Rachel Semon Louis and her parents had lived in Richmond during most of the war, and as the end approached, the older Semons wanted to escape before Union troops arrived. But as Rachel Louis noted, "I had $10,000 worth of tobacco in my rooms and had determined to save it. Then the idea came into my head that as soon as the troops came into town I would hoist the flag, and would be assured protection." Her father believed that she would not dare to do it, but the strong-willed woman thought she had little to lose.

She had embroidered the flag in 1859, and during the war, lest she be thought a traitor, kept the flag concealed behind a mirror. The ruse worked, and although a number of surrounding houses were destroyed, the Semon residence survived intact. But the family lost the tobacco anyway; fearing the Union soldiers would seize it, her husband and father had hired draymen to move it to a safe warehouse, where the great fire consumed it.

And so Rachel Louis, like the other Jews of Virginia, faced the end of the war with little but her determination to begin life anew.

"Giving our all to the poor soldiers:" Jewish Women in the Civil War

Dr. Pamela S. Nadell

"[W]rite…long loving letters…to a Soldier…
whose whole soul is home, home,
Sweet home..."

In February 1862, from Paw Paw, Virginia, Marcus Spiegel wrote these words to his beloved Caroline. Two months earlier he had enlisted in the Union Army. The Spiegels' separation mirrors one of the paramount experiences of women, North and South, Christian and Jew, during the Civil War. As men went off to war, they left behind wives, mothers, and daughters. At home, women, whether of the Union or of the Confederacy – and the greater number of American Jews lived behind Union lines – found themselves shouldering unexpected responsibilities and sharing in the mandate to sustain, in women's ways, their cause. As others have noted, in times of war women and men led very different lives.[1]

rtime hospital
rmory Square,
ependence Avenue
Seventh Street, SW.

Of the more than two million men who fought in the Civil War, only eight to ten thousand were Jews; of these, two to three thousand fought for the Confederacy. Geography fanned "the flame of patriotism." It determined the army to which mothers sent their sons. Richmond's Moses Ezekiel recalled that his mother Catherine "would not own a son who would not fight for his home and country." August Bondi, who served with the Fifth Kansas Cavalry, recalled his mother saying that "as a *Jehudi* [Jew] [he] had the duty…to defend the institutions which gave equal rights to all beliefs."[2]

Northern women suffered neither the "ravages of battle" nor the "material deprivation" Southerners faced as the war and its blockade dragged on, nor did they ever have to face the hostility of an occupying army. As the "Confederate homefront became a world of white women and of slaves," Southern ladies discovered just how much the lives they had known before the war depended on the protection of their fathers, husbands, and sons and on the labor of the slaves their men had managed.[3]

Wartime meant new household responsibilities: weaving, spinning, sewing and knitting for their families and, as Eugenia Levy Phillips expressed, "giving our all to the poor soldiers." It meant new women's organizations – more than a thousand appeared across the South. For some it meant paid employment. For many in the South it meant rage against the Union and against its occupation.[4] In all this, Jewish women took part.

The rare Civil War diary of a Jewish teen living in New Orleans, by far the largest city in the South, offers a glimpse into the world of the Confederacy. Three months after the opening salvo at Fort Sumter, South Carolina, Clara Solomon copied the following from the *Daily Delta* into her new diary: "The time for idle threats and bravado is over. We are in the midst of a great conflict, from which we can not back out if we would. We must conquer or perish. There is no alternative..." Charleston's Phoebe Yates Levy Pember shared Solomon's patriotism. Later Pember would remember the "women of the South had been openly and violently rebellious from the moment they thought their states' rights touched ...They were the first to rebel – the last to succumb." That was certainly true of Ophelia, Emma, and Carrie Mayer. After the occupation of Natchez, Mississippi, they smuggled clothing destined for Confederate soldiers, hanging it over the hoops under their skirts, as they drove past unsuspecting Union guards at the city limits.[5]

Clara Solomon followed the war and its battles closely. Soon, however, her family felt its effects. Clara's father, Solomon Solomon, was called away to supply clothing and equipment to the troops in Virginia, and Clara missed him terribly: "My tears blind me. Oh! God! Answer our prayers & waft to us tidings of him whom our hearts adore."[6]

The economic blockade of the South and the loss of many families' chief breadwinner increased women's burdens. Within a few months, Clara spent her day mending, "renovating" last year's garments. Coffee soared to a dollar a pound. Her mother stretched it with rye and warned that soon they would have to do without.[7]

Meanwhile, the war came closer. Clara joined her teachers and schoolmates packing boxes of bandages, medicines, and preserves to send to the wounded in hospitals. Her "heart ache[d]" as daily she read the "long lists of death." She cried, "This slaughter of human lives – this, this is war; war, with all its horrors." Her growing despair echoed that of Emma Mordecai, half-sister of Rachel Mordecai Lazarus, as she mourned a death in the Petersburg, Virginia, entrenchments, "A true Israelite without guile – a soldier of the Lord & a soldier of the South." As fires raged in the city of Columbia, South Carolina, after its defeat, Eleanor H. Cohen found her family "houseless, homeless, and without food or clothing. In one night we were brought from comparative wealth and luxury to abject poverty. ...I never imagined I should be so near actual starvation."[8]

For Clara Solomon, the fall of New Orleans and its occupation by Yankee troops brought the greatest humiliation. Even while "indispensable articles....from Yankee Land" eased material deprivation, Clara railed against General Benjamin F. Butler's occupation. She confided to her diary: "If he could only have as many ropes around his neck as there are ladies in the city & each have a pull! Or if we could fry him!"[9]

Clara was not the only New Orleans young woman to wish harm to "Beast" Butler. He was ruthless – firing on civilians, hanging a man for destroying a Union flag, seizing the shops of those who refused Yankee business, condemning the rich men of the city to labor in chain gangs – all to bring hostile civilians under control. Nevertheless, the women of New Orleans continued to display anger and hatred toward his men. Consequently, in May 1862, he "ordered that hereafter when any female shall, by word, gesture, or movement, insult or show contempt for any officer or soldier of the United States, she shall be regarded and ... treated as a woman of the town plying her avocation." If the women would not behave like ladies, he would treat them just as they behaved. This insult to the honor of Southern womanhood unleashed a "war upon the women of the land."[10]

Its most famous Jewish victim was Eugenia Levy Phillips, an ardent secessionist who boasted of her Southern sisters, "Our women were all heroines." Employing the rhetorical conventions of her day, she described herself as "only a wretched, weak woman." Nevertheless, this "weak woman," wed at sixteen, bore nine children, was imprisoned twice for her Confederate sympathies, and lived to the age of eighty-one.[11]

When war broke out, the Phillipses lived in Washington. In August 1861, Eugenia was arrested on suspicion of espionage. As soldiers began combing through her home, she whispered to her Irish maid to destroy her correspondence. Nevertheless, for the next three weeks, she and her older daughters were confined to a garret, where these "virtuous, refined, pure-minded women" endured the indignities of being "arrested, searched, shipped, shut up as prisoners." Not one to give in easily to despair, when Eugenia fell ill, she "determined to live to plague mankind a little more and in the hope of seeing a few of these 'detectives' hung."[12]

After her release, the family settled in New Orleans. There, "Beast" Butler arrested her. Eugenia Phillips assumed he would accuse her of raising a subscription for the widow of the man executed for desecrating the Union flag. Instead he charged her with laughing and mocking the funeral procession of a Federal officer. When Eugenia responded that she "was in good spirits" that day, Butler screamed, "I do not call you a common woman of the town, but an uncommonly vulgar one," and he sentenced her to imprisonment on Ship Island, a disease-ridden, bug-infested sandbar off the coast of New Orleans. There, accompanied by her loyal Irish maidservant, Eugenia spent the next three-and-a-half months in tremendous want and deprivation, "treated worse than the vilest felon." Eventually, she was released purportedly "to prevent the sufferings of the *wholly innocent.*" By intimating that Eugenia was pregnant, Butler found a convenient pretext for her release.[13]

Eugenia Levy Phillips was not the only Southern patriot in her family. Her sister Phoebe Yates Levy Pember also served the cause. During the war, women North and South, bereft of breadwinners and living in economies enduring labor shortages, took up paid employment. In the South, women became teachers in far greater numbers than before. For women North and South, the U.S. publication of Florence Nightingale's *Notes on Nursing* in 1860 made female nursing respectable. In September 1862, the Confederate Congress, recognizing the superior care the wounded received when women did the nursing, designated matrons' positions for women in military hospitals. Pember, a thirty-nine-year-old widow, living unhappily with relatives, became matron of hospital number two in the sprawling Chimborazo complex in Richmond, Virginia. By war's end, its 150 wards had treated 76,000 patients.[14]

Pember proved unusual. Southern women of her social class generally eschewed matrons' positions, fearing they would, as she reflected, be "injurious to the delicacy and refinement of a lady." Further, the pain and misery a lady would face and the physically challenging work she would have to perform would cause "her nature [to] become deteriorated and her sensibilities blunted." Nevertheless, as Pember reveals in her memoir *A Southern Woman's Story*, as matron she did what she had to do, keeping house, cooking, and nursing thousands of men over the next several years. Not surprisingly, this first female administrator at Chimborazo encountered opposition from those who resented female authority, among them the surgeons who wanted to dispense whiskey's medicine by themselves and often for themselves.[15]

Pember shared her compatriots' hatred of the Yankees. Describing an evening spent among "good Christians" excoriating the enemy, where one woman asked her for a "Yankee Skull to keep her toilet trinkets in," Pember explained that she took refuge in

> being born of a nation, and religion that did not enjoin forgiveness on its enemies, that enjoyed the blessed privilege of praying for an eye for an eye, and a life for a life, and was not one of those for whom Christ died in vain...I proposed that till the war was over they should all join the Jewish church. ...It was a very agreeable evening...I certainly had the best of the argument.[16]

As the war turned against the Confederacy, the situation at Chimborazo became increasingly desperate. When Richmond was evacuated in April 1865, Pember stayed on determined to do her duty. In the chaos of the withdrawal, when "hospital rats" tried to steal her whiskey, the stalwart matron met them with pistol cocked in her pocket. Pember continued to nurse the sick until all "were either convalescent or dead, and at last my vocation was gone."[17]

In many ways, the women's wartime experiences in the North mirrored those in the South. Women North and South "trembled in suspense and fear," as did Caroline Spiegel, "to learn of [the] fate" of their loved ones. Northern women too nursed the wounded, although no Northern Jewish woman left a record of wartime nursing to match that of Phoebe Pember. Yet, when Union General Charles H. T. Collis had pneumonia, Septima Levy Collis managed to get permission to go to the front in Culpeper, Virginia, to nurse her husband.[18]

Northern women also organized for soldiers' aid. But, with larger numbers of Jewish women in the North, they sometimes did so in distinctively Jewish groups in the tradition of the benevolent societies, which were by now a well-established part of Jewish communal life. As war broke out, "the Ladies of the Congregation, Shearith Israel" prepared "to assist the families of their fellow-citizens, who have volunteered in defense of their country, its constitution and laws." In Philadelphia, the Ladies Hebrew Association for the Relief of Sick and Wounded Union Soldiers sought "to obviate the sufferings of the brave soldiers ... while they lie in the army hospitals ...irrespective of religious creed." In New York, Boston, and Chicago, Jewish women rolled bandages together and packed boxes for the wounded. At New York's Temple Emanu-El, they sewed uniforms.[19]

Their soldiers' aid work formed but a tiny part of a far-reaching network of Northern women massed to help sustain "the largest military operation on American soil." Just as men from every sector of the Union responded to the call to defend the nation, so too women from all over the North, Christian and Jew, the well-to-do and those struggling to make ends meet, did their part for the cause. Much of this women's work was coordinated through the United States Sanitary Commission, established by the federal government in 1861 to centralize, as much as possible, local relief efforts. Philadelphia's Ladies Hebrew Association for the Relief of Sick and Wounded Union Soldiers appointed Matilda Cohen its representative to the Commission.[20]

In addition to directing the dispensing of supplies and medicines, the Commission also promoted, starting in the fall of 1863, fundraising events called sanitary fairs. They were modeled on women's antebellum charity and church fairs, among them Jewish women's modest fairs, like the one held in 1857 to benefit Philadelphia's Jewish Foster Home. Thanks to the urging of the Sanitary Commission, during the Civil War, "fair mania" took hold,[21] with blockbuster fairs in some cities raising enormous sums for relief. Charging admission, selling homemade goods – pin cushions, potholders, and pencil cases – offering refreshments and entertainments like art exhibitions and Indian dances, these spectacles welcomed wide participation and gave women, especially those of the middle and upper classes, a crucial venue for displaying their patriotism.

Jewish women stood side-by-side with their neighbors at these fairs. New York's 1864 Metropolitan Fair included Jewish representatives on all its organizing committees. At a Sanitary Fair in Cincinnati in 1863, the Jewish community set up four stands including one run by the "Independent Ladies." At Washington, D.C.'s Sanitary Fair in 1864, the Hebrew Society's Table raised $756.95, almost one-tenth of the total receipts for the day. "All honor to our fair Jewesses!" reported the Jewish press with obvious pride.[22]

For many women in the North, however, as for those in the South, their paramount experience of war was not a sanitary fair, but rather the absence of their men. Surely, Caroline Frances Hamlin Spiegel's experiences were typical. She tried to ease her husband's life in the field. The Quaker who had learned German cooking to become a Jewess sent her immigrant husband a box filled with goose meat, pfeffernüsse (peppernut cookies) and "zuker" (sugar) cookies. She arranged to have a family portrait taken so that Marcus could gaze upon his loved ones. For his part Marcus managed to secure a furlough in time to be with Caroline during the birth of their fourth child; a subsequent leave left her pregnant.[23]

Septima Maria Levy Collis, born in Charleston, South Carolina, "became a *Union* woman by marrying a Northern soldier." To her dismay, the war caused him to miss the birth of their first child. While their early wartime separation was not atypical for a soldier's family, Septima Collis's later wartime experiences, recounted in a "few brief incidents of my army life," were rather unusual. Because of her husband's rank – eventually he rose to major general – she and her daughter were permitted to join him in the field. There the Northerner by marriage who mourned the battlefield death of her brother, the Confederate lieutenant David Cardoza Levy, generally found life at headquarters, among the wives of the other generals, including Mrs. Ulysses S. Grant, "very gay ... with dinners, balls, reviews, races, and calvacades..." Once, Septima Collis even came under fire as she rode out with her orderly. Later she was "quite proud" to have entered the "beleaguered city" of Richmond just after its evacuation.[24]

The war also presented Yankee women with new economic and political challenges: they assumed greater autonomy in running their households.[25] Caroline Spiegel was no exception.

Now she shared in managing the family finances; she asked Marcus about money he was owed and how she should go about getting it. He wrote of how much of his Army pay he was sending home. Septima Levy Collis too recalled how "expensive" things were, and how after an officer had "paid for his 'mess' and his servant, there was little left for his family at home."[26]

The war also compelled Northern women to deal with government officials in new ways. Marcus Spiegel, unable to accomplish what he wanted from his post in the field, asked his wife to intercede for him to get a command in a new regiment. To a private audience with President Lincoln, Septima Collis wore a "pale-pearl silk dress … immense hoops … a long train … lace shawl … pearl-colored bonnet … [and] illusion veil," remembering years later every detail of her dress for that momentous occasion as she asked the president to promote her husband. When Lincoln responded that he was too young, Mrs. Collis replied, "He is not too young to be killed in the service, and make me a widow."[27]

For the Spiegels, the wartime separation challenged the marriage. Caroline confessed that she had "the blues." Marcus recognized "the Heroism" his wife required "to lead the life" she was "compelled to live" since he went into the army. When the heroine pleaded for the soldier to resign his commission and come home, the colonel lectured on duty to country and wished his wife were "a little more incoraging [*sic*] as to [his] military career."[28] Caroline was not alone in wishing her husband would leave the battlefield. Historians find Union husbands and wives arguing over "priorities as women asked men to come home and men lectured women on the imperatives of national duty."[2]

War's end signified different things for Jewish women depending on where they stood in the years of the War between the States. Southerners like Emma Mordecai, despairing over defeat and war's ravages, felt "as if there was nothing more to live for in this world."[30] Surely, many, North and South, heaved a collective sigh of relief. During the war Philadelphian Rebecca Gratz felt "constant agitation" over the fate of loved ones on both sides of the divide. Now she could cease her worrying.[31] But for many, many others, Caroline Hamlin Spiegel among them, surrender brought no respite from her sorrows. War's end left her a soldier's widow with four children. She was forced to turn to Washington Jewish communal leader Simon Wolf to help her secure the pension the U.S. Government gave to the families of those who had made the greatest sacrifices of all in the war fought "to make men free."[32]

1 Marcus M. Spiegel, Frank L. Byrne, ed., and Jean Powers Soman, eds., *Your True Marcus: The Civil War Letters of a Jewish Colonel* (Kent, Ohio: Kent State University Press, 1985), 51. Little is written about Jewish women and the Civil War; see Hasia R. Diner, "Civil War in the United States," in *Jewish Women in America: A Comprehensive Historical Encyclopedia (CD-ROM)*, ed. Paula E. Hyman and Dalia Ofer (Jerusalem: Shalvi Publishing, 2006); Drew Gilpin Faust, *Mothers of Invention: Women of the Slaveholding South in the American Civil War* (Chapel Hill: University of North Carolina Press, 1996), 10.
2 "American Civil War." *Encyclopædia Britannica*. 2008. Encyclopædia Britannica Online. Accessed 22 Mar. 2008, http:// www.search.eb.com.proxyau.wrlc.org/eb/article-229879; Jonathan D. Sarna, *American Judaism: A History* (New Haven: Yale University Press, 2004), 113; Robert N. Rosen, *The Jewish Confederates* (Columbia: University of South Carolina Press, 2000), 162, 50; Elliott Ashkenazi, ed., *The Civil War Diary of Clara Solomon: Growing up in New Orleans, 1861-1862* (Baton Rouge: Louisiana State University Press, 1995), 322; August Bondi, *Autobiography of August Bondi*, excerpted in Jacob Rader Marcus, ed., *Memoirs of American Jews, 1775-1865* (New York: Ktav, 1974), vol. 2, 203.
3 Faust, *Mothers of Invention*, 31, 5-7.
4 Ibid., 49, 24, 197-98; Eugenia Levy Phillips, "Defiant Rebel," in *Memoirs of American Jews, 1775-1865*, ed. Jacob Rader Marcus (1955; rpt. New York: Ktav, 1974), 161-96, 179.
5 Ashkenazi, ed., *The Civil War Diary of Clara Solomon*, 77. Pember quoted in Robert N. Rosen, "Jewish Confederates," in *Jewish Roots in Southern Soil*, ed. Marcie Cohen Ferris and Mark I. Greenberg (Hanover, NH: Brandeis University Press/University Press of New England, 2006), 109-133, 114; cited in Jacob Rader Marcus, ed., *The American Jewish Woman: A Documentary History* (Cincinnati: American Jewish Archives, 1981), 257.
6 Ashkenazi, ed., *The Civil War Diary of Clara Solomon, 1861-1862*, 79, 84, 3, 335.
7 Ibid., 350, 233.
8 Ibid., 334-35, 341, 323. Quoted in Rosen, *The Jewish Confederates*, 199. On Emma

Mordecai's wartime experiences, see Dianne Ashton, "Shifting Veils: Religion, Politics, and Womanhood in the Civil War Writings of American Jewish Women," in *Women and American Judaism: Historical Perspectives*, ed. Pamela S. Nadell and Jonathan D. Sarna (Hanover, NH: Brandeis University Press, 2001), 81-106, 86-89; Quoted in Belinda and Richard Gergel, *In Pursuit of the Tree of Life: A History of the Early Jews of Columbia, South Carolina, and the Tree of Life Congregation*
(Columbia, SC: Tree of Life Congregation, 1996), 41.
9 Ashkenazi, ed., *The Civil War Diary of Clara Solomon*, 419-20.
10 Phillips, "Defiant Rebel," 191. General Order No. 28 quoted in Faust, *Mothers of Invention*, 208-10.
11 Phillips, "Defiant Rebel," 188.
12 Ibid., 170, 168.
13 Ibid., 189, 194.
14 Faust, *Mothers of Invention*, 82, 97-98. For example, Clara Solomon's sister Alice was already teaching in a girls' public elementary school, and Clara was studying to become a teacher; Ashkenazi, ed., *The Civil War Diary of Clara Solomon,* 5-6; Rosen, *The Jewish Confederates*, 297.
15 Pember quoted in Faust, *Mothers of Invention*, 98-101; Rosen, *The Jewish Confederates*, 296-303.
16 Pember letter quoted in Rosen, *The Jewish Confederates*, 300.
17 Pember quoted in Ibid., 303.
18 Spiegel, Byrne, and Soman, *Your True Marcus*, 226; Septima Maria Levy Collis, *A Woman's War Record, 1861-1865* (1889; reprint, http://docsouth.unc.edu/fpn/collis/collis.html; accessed 15 May 2008), 23.
19 Newspaper account of the Ladies Hebrew Association for the Relief of Sick and Wounded Union Soldiers," 26 June 1863, in Marcus, ed., *The American Jewish Woman*, 246-47; Philip S. Foner, *The Jews in American History, 1654-1865* (New York: International Publishers, 1945), 70-71; Diner, "Civil War in the United States."
20 On the women's work cutting "across class, ethnic, and religious lines" and on the U.S. Sanitary Commission, see Nina Silber, *Daughters of the Union: Northern Women Fight the Civil War* (Cambridge: Harvard University Press, 2005), 163, 173, 176-193; Diner, "Civil War in the United States."
21 Barbara Kirshenblatt-Gimblett, "The Moral Sublime: Jewish Women and Philanthropy in Nineteenth-Century America," in *Writing a Modern Jewish History: Essays in Honor of Salo W. Baron*, ed. Barbara Kirshenblatt-Gimblett (New York and New Haven: The Jewish Museum and Yale University Press, 2006), 36-54, 38; Silber, *Daughters of the* Union, 185.
22 Kirshenblatt-Gimblett, "The Moral Sublime: Jewish Women and Philanthropy in Nineteenth-Century America," 41; Silber, *Daughters of the Union*, 163.
The United States Sanitary Commission, formed in 1861, coordinated this work.
23 Spiegel, Byrne, and Soman, *Your True Marcus*, 56, 268, 109, 292, 311.
24 Collis, *A Woman's War Record, 1861-1865*, 17, 32-33, 46, 54, 58.
25 Silber, *Daughters of the Union*, 9.
26 Spiegel, Byrne, and Soman, *Your True Marcus*, 129; Collis, *A Woman's War Record, 1861-1865*, 16.
27 Silber, *Daughters of the Union*, 9; Spiegel, Byrne, and Soman, *Your True Marcus*, 129-30, 170-71; Collis, *A Woman's War Record, 1861-1865*, 19-22.
28 Spiegel, Byrne, and Soman, *Your True Marcus*, 136, 276, 285, 289.
29 Silber, *Daughters of the Union*, 26.
30 Quoted in Myron Berman, *Richmond's Jewry, 1769-1976* (Charlottesville: University Press of Virginia for the Jewish Community Federation of Richmond, 1979), 196-97.
31 Ashton, "Shifting Veils," 100.
32 Spiegel, Byrne, and Soman, *Your True Marcus*, 338. The closing words are from Julia Ward Howe's "Battle Hymn of the Republic," 1861.

Ulysses S. Grant and the Jews: An Unsolved Mystery

Dr. John Y. Simon

A president of the United States still remembered for a disgraceful public act of antisemitism attended the dedication of Adas Israel Congregation's building in Washington, D.C., in 1876. After separating from the Washington Hebrew Congregation in 1869 in search of a more traditional mode of worship, the founders of Adas Israel occupied temporary quarters until 1876, when they launched a campaign to complete a synagogue before July 4, the centennial of American independence. On June 9, President Ulysses S. Grant, his son Ulysses, Jr., a recent Harvard graduate who had become his father's secretary, and Senator Thomas W. Ferry of Michigan, president pro tempore of the Senate and consequently first in line to succeed President Grant since the death of Vice-President Henry Wilson, took seats in the synagogue. Methodist Episcopal Bishop John P. Newman accompanied the party, perhaps to

ortly after his election, esident Grant posed for athew Brady in 1869.

chaperone the Methodist president. Grant reportedly made a cash contribution at the conclusion of the dedicatory ceremonies.

Fourteen years earlier, Major General Grant had been guilty of a shocking display of antisemistism. On December 17, 1862, he issued General Orders No. 11:

> I. The Jews, as a class, violating every regulation of trade established by the Treasury Department, and also Department orders, are hereby expel[led] from the Department.
>
> II. Within twenty-four hours from the receipt of this order by Post Commanders, they will see that all of this class of people are furnished with passes and required to leave, and any one returning after such notifications, will be arrested and held in confinement until an opportunity occurs of sending them out as prisoners unless furnished with permits from these Head Quarters.
>
> III. No permits will be given these people to visit Head Quarters for the purpose of making personal application for trade permits.

Why did Grant issue such an order? This mystery has only a partial solution.

By December 17, Grant had advanced along the line of the Mississippi Central Railroad as far as Oxford. From there, he instructed General William T. Sherman to lead an expedition down the Mississippi River to Vicksburg, the ultimate objective of Grant's campaign. Grant knew that his army had advanced deep into Mississippi with a tenuous supply line, while enemy forces remained intact and mobile, and that his divided armies risked fighting superior Confederate forces. Given such strategic anxieties, he could hardly be expected to devote thought to matters of trade. But such concerns constantly intruded.

The outbreak of war had so increased the value of cotton in the North and in Europe that planters continued to grow it despite a Confederate embargo. By the end of 1862, Grant's advance carried him toward the richest plantations, some storing harvests from two growing seasons.

A confused and ambivalent U.S. Government trade policy provided generous loopholes for the enterprising and unscrupulous. When war began, Secretary of the Treasury Salmon P. Chase moved immediately to halt the shipping of "munitions of war" to the Confederacy, but not until four months later did President Abraham Lincoln give the Treasury authority to regulate trade with insurrectionary regions. Chase believed that trade should follow the flag, so as armies moved southward, Treasury agents gave permits to loyal citizens to resume normal commerce. Such a policy would reconcile citizens to the federal government and benefit the Northern economy through the flow of needed Southern products.

What looked sound and sensible from Washington looked disgraceful from army headquarters in Mississippi, where everyone knew how often goods traded by "loyal" persons behind the lines seeped southward to the Confederacy in exchange for cotton. The war had cut off the supply of cotton to New England mills and the world market, raising customary prices. The government expected the army to seize captured and abandoned cotton for sale to benefit the Treasury, thus defraying the staggering cost of war and ending the cotton famine. But as the army advanced, patriotic Confederates burned their cotton rather than lose their hoards. Some rebels, aware of the imminent arrival of the enemy and reluctant to torch their only capital asset, pursued an alternative. Traders or their agents who slipped through the lines offered gold, weapons, or medicine in return for these doomed bales. Such illegal and unpatriotic practices were lucrative enough to warrant the risk. Speculators who bought cotton could profit enough to enable them to bribe officers and officials to look away or even to assist as they smuggled cotton through the lines.

Wartime cotton trade in the Mississippi Valley outraged patriotic Northerners, soldiers and civilians alike. Unscrupulous traders enabled Confederates to fight more effectively by supplying gold and scarce goods, deprived the U.S. Treasury of revenue, and corrupted the military. Officers and journalists frequently blamed this trade on Jews.

When war began, some 150,000 Jews lived in the United States. About two-thirds were born abroad and had crossed the Atlantic for much the same reasons as other recent immigrants. Like them, Jews more often settled in the North than in the South, and disproportionately in cities. Whether they were disproportionate participants in the wartime cotton trade cannot be determined, but contemporaries wrote as if they were. An 1863 investigation of cotton-buying in the Mississippi Valley involved hundreds of soldiers and civilians, only four of them Jewish. Some ugly remarks about "Jew traders" may have been intended as insults to non-Jewish traders. Unfortunately, these actions strengthened the impression that Jews dominated the cotton business.

Like their fellow citizens, Jews enlisted in local regiments when the war began. Ultimately, approximately 8,000 to 10,000 Jewish soldiers served North and South. When Grant issued General Orders No. 11, the highest-ranking Jewish officer in his command, Lieutenant Colonel Marcus M. Spiegel, 120th Ohio, son of a German rabbi, was with his regiment on Sherman's expedition to Vicksburg.

Grant's imperial Department of the Tennessee stretched from northern Mississippi to Cairo, Illinois, and from the Mississippi River to the Tennessee River. Within this domain, he delegated administrative duties to subordinates while concentrating his attention on the armies moving southward. But he could not ignore civil problems in his department. Both Grant and Sherman vehemently, but fruitlessly, protested prevailing trade regulations that encouraged fraud and corruption. Constantly vexed by the cotton trade, Grant fell prey to the pervasive antisemitism of the day.

On July 26, 1862, Grant telegraphed an officer at Columbus, Kentucky: "Examine the baggage of all speculators coming South, and, when they [have] specie, turn them back. If medicine and other contraband articles, arrest them and confiscate the contraband articles. Jews should receive special attention." On November 9, he telegraphed Memphis: "Refuse all permits to come south of Jackson for the present[.] The Israelites especially should be kept out[.]" The following day, Grant instructed his superintendent of military railroads to "Give orders to all the conductors…on the road that no Jews are to be permitted to travel on the Rail road southward from any point[.] They may go north and be encouraged in it but they are such an intolerable nuisance that the Department must be purged for them[.]" Yet when Colonel John Van Deusen Du Bois issued orders on December 8 expelling "Cotton-Speculators, Jews and other Vagrants" from Holly Springs, Grant immediately ordered them revoked as violating instructions from Washington encouraging cotton shipping from the South.

Grant's prompt revocation of Du Bois's order makes more puzzling his issuance of similar orders within a few days. Timing suggests that Grant's rage was ignited by the arrival of his father in Mississippi to buy cotton for a Jewish firm in Cincinnati in return for one-quarter of the profits. Jesse R. Grant was no simpleton ensnared by crafty speculators. A shrewd businessman, he rose from poverty to affluence through aggressive business practices. A neighbor remembered him as willing "to follow a dollar to hell."

Jesse's relationship with his son was complex. It was the father who had arranged his son's appointment to West Point and then forced him to attend. When Ulysses resigned from the army fifteen years later, his father-in-law, rather than his father, tried to help him establish a farm. When necessity eventually drove Grant to his father's leather store in Galena, Illinois, he worked for a younger brother for a less-than-generous salary.

Jesse's attempt to use his paternity as a source of cotton profits was the last straw. On the eve of his father's arrival, Ulysses complained of "speculators whose patriotism is measured by dollars and cents. Country has no value with them compared to money." Suddenly he realized that his father fit this condemnation. Perhaps displacing his anger, Grant lashed out at his father's Jewish partners. Grant's ire appeared even more clearly in a letter, written the day he issued the orders, to Assistant Secretary of War Christopher P. Wolcott:

> I have long since believed that in spite of all the vigilance that can be infused into Post Commanders that the Specie regulations of the Treasury Dept. have been violated, and that mostly by Jews and other unprincipled traders. So well satisfied of this have I been that I instructed the Commdg Officer at Columbus to refuse all permits to Jews to come south, and frequently have had them expelled from the Dept. But they come in with their Carpet sacks in spite of all that can be done to prevent it. The Jews seem to be a privileged class that can travel anywhere.

Grant's senseless reference in his orders to Jews as a "class" created considerable confusion in enforcement. Several officers asked whether these orders applied to Jewish sutlers, the licensed traders who accompanied regiments. At least one Jewish officer resigned. Captain Philip Trounstine, Fifth Ohio Cavalry, explained that he was "either fortunately or unfortunately born of Jewish parents," that he owed "filial affection to my parents, Devotion to my Religion, and a deep regard for the opinion of my friends" and could "no longer, bear the taunts and malice, of those whom my religious opinions are known[.]"

Information about enforcement within the Department of the Tennessee remains hazy, but the orders were zealously enforced at Paducah, Kentucky, where Jews were expelled on 24-hours' notice. Entire families were driven from their homes. Two women lying ill were exempted; two army veterans were not. In his inaugural address in 1869, President Grant would later state, "I know no method to secure the repeal of bad or obnoxious laws so effective as their stringent execution." Nowhere had this become more effectively demonstrated than in Paducah, where Jewish leaders began a protest eventually heard in Washington.

Cesar F. Kaskel of Paducah, barred from telegraphing Grant, wired Lincoln. He then proceeded toward Washington, along the way visiting or writing to Jewish leaders to create pressure for revocation. Kaskel headed toward the right man. During the 1850s, Lincoln had flatly rejected any political advantage through harnessing prejudice.

After meeting Kaskel, Lincoln wrote a note to Major General Henry W. Halleck, who sent Grant a characteristically cautious telegram: "A paper purporting to be a Genl Order No. 11 issued by you Dec 17th has been presented here. By its terms it expels all Jews from your Dept. If such an order has been issued, it will be immediately revoked. On the following day, Halleck's aide, Colonel John C. Kelton, wrote to Grant: "Permit me to inform you unofficially the objection taken to your Genl Order No 11. It excluded a whole class, instead of certain obnoxious individuals. Had the word 'peddler' been inserted after Jew I do not suppose any exception would have been taken to the order. Several officers and a number of enlisted men in your Dept are Jews. A Govr of one of the Western states is a Jew."

Kelton presumably meant Governor Edward Salomon of Wisconsin, who was a Lutheran. Halleck himself wrote to Grant on January 21 that the "President has no objection to your expelling traders and Jew pedlars, which I suppose was the object of your order, but as it in terms prescribed an entire religious class, some of whom are fighting in our ranks, the President deemed it necessary to revoke it."

After Grant revoked the orders, Congress tabled censure resolutions introduced into the House and Senate. General Orders No. 11 might then have been forgotten had its author not entered politics.

The Orders received more newspaper coverage in 1868 than when first issued. After Grant's presidential nomination, Democratic newspapers revived the issue, urging Jewish voters, then customarily Republican, to switch allegiance. Democratic attacks inspired Republican excuses. Had Grant acted on orders from Washington? This theory was first advanced in 1863 by Jesse Grant and in newspapers. Accounts of Grant's instructions contradicted one another. However, no documentary evidence existed that would absolve Grant of responsibility.

Had Assistant Secretary of War Wolcott or someone else in Washington expressed the antisemitism reflected in General Orders No. 11, giving Grant encouragement when he lashed out at cotton traders? Although not writing as one obeying orders, Grant explained his actions to Wolcott in his December 17th letter. Wolcott was a man to whom Grant had never addressed any communication previously.

Grant partisans tried other postwar political explanations for the embarrassing order, shifting blame to a staff officer or some other subordinate. Since Grant's other communications concerning Jews remained unpublicized, this seemed plausible. But as election passions heated, this excuse failed. Grant could not disclaim personal responsibility. Instead, he wrote to an old friend who had forwarded a letter from a concerned Jewish voter:

> I do not pretend to sustain the order. At the time of its publication I was insensed [sic.] by a reprimand received from Washington for permitting acts which the Jews, within my lines, were engaged in. There were many others within my lines equally bad with the worst of them, but the difference was that the Jews could pass with impunity, from one Army to the other. Gold, in violation of orders, was being smuggled through the lines by them. At least so it was reported. The order was made and sent out, without any reflection, and without thinking of the Jews as a sect or race to themselves, but simply as the persons who had successfully (I say successfully instead of persistently because I know there were a plenty within my lines who envied them their success) violated an order, which violation inured greatly to the help of the rebels...I have no prejudice against sect or race but want each individual to be judged by his own merit. Order No. 11 does not sustain this statement, I admit, but then I do not sustain that order. It never would have been issued if it had not been telegraphed the moment penned, without one moments reflection.

Grant's rambling letter, however, did not explain his earlier instructions concerning Jews. His defensive tone indicates Grant had not yet grasped the enormity of his offense.

Campaign pressure forced Grant to write something for publication on a topic he did not want to discuss, and through the remainder of his life he maintained public silence about his expulsion of the Jews. Grant's wife, however, remembered his speaking of "that obnoxious order" and of the Congressional resolutions that he said were deserved "as he had no right to make an order against any special sect."

Grant had occupied the White House for less than six weeks when he received a visit from Rabbi H.Z. Sneersohn of Jerusalem, a proto-Zionist who traveled around the globe promoting settlement in Palestine. In January 1870, Sneersohn wrote to "the chosen Chieftain of the United States of America, warrior, hero and prince of peace, Ulysses S. Grant," thanking him for his assistance to the Jews of Jerusalem and calling his attention to the persecution of Jews in Romania. He asked that a consul be sent to Romania sympathetic to the Jews, preferably someone Jewish, and asked pardon, "mighty ruler, beneficent chieftain, beloved of God and of men – pardon a stranger of a strange land – …if his cries disturb thee in thy labors and rob thee of the precious time which belongs to the government of thy good people…" Grant received confirmation of the Romanian persecutions from others, including Abraham Hart, president of the Board of Delegates of American Israelites.

Grant appointed Benjamin F. Peixotto, formerly an editor of the *Cleveland Plain Dealer* and grand master of B'nai B'rith, later a lawyer in San Francisco, as a consul to Bucharest. Peixotto carried with him a letter from Grant explaining that

> Mr[.] Peixotto has undertaken the duties of his present office more as a missionary work for the benefit of the people who are laboring under severe oppression than for any benefits to accrue to himself, a work which all good citizens will wish him the greatest success in. The United States knowing no distinction of her own citizens on account of religion or nativity naturally believe in a civilization the world over which will secure the same universal liberal views.

Grant had already received a petition from Simon Wolf and others regarding persecution of Jews in Russia and had responded that "in this age of enlightenment it is too late in the day to persecute any one on account of condition, birth, creed, or color." Without adequately apologizing for his wartime orders, Grant had shown sufficient concern for the plight of Jews abroad to appease critics at home. Under those circumstances, Adas Israel welcomed Grant to its dedication. The deeper significance of the occasion lay in what remained unspoken between the president and those he had previously so deeply offended, but his presence alone reaffirmed his well-known maxim: "Let us have peace."

WASHINGTON
HEBREW
CONGREGATION

The Jewish Community of Washington, D.C., during the Civil War

Robert Shosteck

INTRODUCTION

Washington, D.C., is unique among American cities in that it is both a city and the capital of the United States. Throughout its long history, the city has been made up of two segments: permanent residents of the city whose roots were in Washington, and a smaller but influential segment whose roots were elsewhere. These were the politicians and their staffs, the lobbyists, and those whose business with the government required their sojourn for a few months or a few years.

During war times – and this was particularly true of the Civil War period – these transient residents increased in number many fold. Many were attracted by business opportunities, the

shington Hebrew Congregation
chased this former Methodist church
ighth and I Streets, NW, in 1863, and
verted it to synagogue use.

chance to earn a good livelihood by meeting the added demand for merchandise and services of all sorts.

These observations regarding the community at large are pertinent for the Jewish community. The Civil War period saw a substantial increase in the size of the Jewish community. Most of these newcomers came for the "duration" and retained their ties in New York and other northern cities. We find it particularly difficult to identify many of these as Jews because their names do not often appear in congregational records. Some able and devoted men and women among these transients made significant contributions to the life of the community.[1]

I. RELIGIOUS ACTIVITIES

Washington Hebrew Congregation was the center of Jewish religious life in the nation's capital during the Civil War period. It was organized on April 25, 1852, at the home of Herman Lissberger on Pennsylvania Avenue near 21st Street.[2] Solomon Pribram was chosen president of the new group. The twenty or more founders were almost all recent immigrants from Germany. Two years later the Congregation had increased to about forty and included Capt. Jonas P. Levy among its supporters.[3]

The growing congregation soon was faced with the problem of finding a suitable place of worship. The editor of *The Occident* reported on the matter as follows:

> We learn from the *Evening Star* that the Israelites are making strenuous exertions to provide themselves with a suitable place of worship. They are highly spoken of for their industry and general good conduct, and have won the good opinion of other denominations. They lately celebrated the receipt of a Sepher Torah, on which occasion they had a public dinner. We trust, however, to hear before many months have elapsed, that the contemplated Synagogue has been completed, and is the resort of many and devout and pious Israelites.[4]

Later in the same year Reverend Isaac Leeser visited Washington and reported on the state of congregational affairs to his readers:

> We visited the house lately fitted up as a place of worship... They have a Hazan and Shochet in the person of the Rev. Mr. H. Melle. We learned...that...several Israelites in the District had not joined the Congregation; but we hope that the difficulties... may be speedily removed, so that the Israelites of the vicinity may contribute, to promote the welfare of their faith.[5]

In July 1857, a constitution and by-laws were formally adopted, and Captain Jonas Levy was elected president.[6] By 1859, the growing congregation had secured a building to serve as their place of worship. A local newspaper describes the event as follows:

> The ceremony of moving into a new synagogue, at the corner of Ninth and D streets, took place on Friday afternoon, May 20 (Iyar 5619) with a full attendance of its members. The usual ceremony was performed by the Rev. Mr. Lansburgh, minister of the Congregation, after which Capt. Jonas P. Levy made a...short address to the audience.[7]

Within a month the congregation was seeking its first paid functionary. The following ad appeared in *The Occident*, in June 1859:

> Wanted: By the first Hebrew Congregation of the City of Washington, a Hazan, Shochet and Teacher in Hebrew, and, if possible, in the German language. The salary will be $400 a year, besides perquisites amounting to $150. Communications, with testimonials must be forwarded to
>
> SAMUEL HERMAN, *Secretary*

By October 1860, the Congregation was looking for larger quarters for its growing membership. A news item tells this story:

> Six years ago there was not a Minyan to be found in that city; now there are about four hundred Yehudim there...great credit should be accorded to Capt. Jonas P. Levy. [8]

When the congregation adopted a Constitution in 1861, it prescribed an "Aschkeness" [*sic*] *Minhag* according to the Redelheim prayer book.[9] S. Weil, elected *hazzan* in 1859, served in that office until 1869. This Constitution provided for salaried officers consisting of "Hazan, Schocath, [*sic*] and Teacher in German and Hebrew. Preacher and Lecturer, if desired." The early war years witnessed the comings and goings of many "Israelites" to and from the nation's capital. The influx of soldiers, the tide of battle, and the burgeoning of war activities in the federal government all attracted newcomers, many Jews among them. As one writer put it,

> So rapid are the changes in Jewish population on the one hand, and the increase so great on the other, that what would be true this year, would be the reverse in the next.[10]

The wartime growth of the Jewish community brought about a need for a larger house of worship. The congregation purchased a church property on 8th Street, NW, between H and I, for $8,000. It was acquired February 9, 1863, by Joseph H. Hanlein, Emanuel Gutman, and Moses Siegel, Trustees of the Congregation.[11] An advertisement appealing for funds appeared in *The Occident*:

> To the Benevolent of Every Sect. The first (and only) Hebrew congregation of the City of Washington...ventures to the benevolent citizens of said city and other cities and places for aid...they have long earnestly desired...a building in which they could...humbly and devoutly worship God; yet the smallness of their number (they are only sixty members...) puts it wholly out of their power to gratify this long cherished desire. But the time has come...to attempt its gratification. They have accordingly entered into a contract for the purchase of a church edifice... from their slender means they have cheerfully contributed several thousand dollars. They earnestly and imploringly ask of the benevolent of the land to aid them in raising the additional amount, to enable them to pay the residue of the said purchase.
>
> Isaac Herzberg, *President*
> Adolph Adler, *Recording Secretary*
>
> J. H. Hanlein
> Emanuel Gutman } *Trustees*[12]
> Moses Siegel

This appeal was endorsed by the Mayor of Washington, as follows:

> Mayor's Office, Washington,
>
> Feb. 17, 1863
>
> This object is a laudable one, which commends itself to all. The parties engaged in the undertaking are residents of this city, personally well known to me, and are gentlemen of character.
>
> RICHARD WALLACH, *Mayor*

The new synagogue was dedicated on July 31, 1863. *The Occident*[13] devoted thirteen pages of its next issue to a description of the ceremonies and summaries of the addresses of the Reverends Isaac Leeser and Henry Hochheimer. Reverend Leeser delivered the principal address, while Reverend Hochheimer, of Baltimore, delivered a short farewell address in German in the old synagogue.

Another newspaper account states that:

> The dedication took place in the presence of a large audience. Several of the clergy of the District were present, among them Revs. W. M. D. Ryan of the M. E. Church, and C. T. Cochel and Oliver Cox of the M. P. Church, and S. P. Hill of the Baptist Church; also many prominent citizens, including members of our City Council, members of the bar and the press.[14]

From the description of the dedication ceremonies, the Congregation's ritual and practices were traditional in character. Until the late 1860s, men and women sat separately at services, and services were held on both the first and second days of holy days.[15]

The Jewish Messenger described a typical service:

> The services were conducted with decorum and solemnity. The Rev. S[amuel] Weil read the services in a devout and agreeable manner, reciting the prayer for the Government in both Hebrew and English. The Haphtorah is read in German... The Congregation is prospering greatly, numbering about ninety members.[16]

Simon Wolf notes that:

> The attendance in synagogue during Passover has been very large. There were but a few soldiers present, owing, I presume, to the difficulty of obtaining passes. The very excellent choir has undergone an orthodox change in the substituting of boys for sopranos, in place of young ladies – a commendable alteration.[17]

The death of Lincoln evoked a great expression of grief in which American Jewry declared its unity with the nation in this time of sorrow. The Reverend Isaac Leeser came to Washington to conduct a memorial service for the late President Lincoln. This event was reported in *The Occident*:

> The Editor was called on...to deliver an address on the 22d of April with reference to the death of President Lincoln. Not deeming himself at liberty to refuse the request, he repaired thither...and spoke on Verse 3, of Chapter 10, of Leviticus... the Synagogue was about two-thirds full, many Israelites in the city being too much absorbed in business to devote this one day to the service of God in the first place, and to do honor to the memory of the President...those present, however, proved by the close attention to the service that they felt the importance of the occasion.[18]

Leeser also chided the local community for its lack of observance of the Sabbath:

> As regards the Israelites of Washington, they are generally prosperous; but we deeply regret that the Sabbath rest is so generally neglected by far too many. They speak of reforming this wrong, and we hope that they may have the heart to keep their promises, and that others may soon join them in their good change.[19]

II. SOCIAL AND CULTURAL LIFE

The organization of a congregation and the steady growth of the Jewish community of Washington led to the development of purely Jewish social and cultural groups.

A fraternal group, the Free Sons of Israel, is mentioned briefly as early as 1857:

> Pursuant to a call by the Sons of Israel…a meeting was held at the Synagogue on Fourth Street, on Sunday evening, the 20th of September, 1857. Captain Jonas P. Levy was called to the chair, and Mr. Levy Bar as Secretary.

The purpose of this meeting was to protest against the Swiss Treaty, which discriminated against American Jewish citizens sojourning there.[20] We do not hear again about the Free Sons of Israel in periodicals until after the Civil War, when the local branch, known as Isaiah Lodge No. 22, is listed in *Boyd's Directory* for 1869.

Some Jews took an active role in fraternal groups and in societies. Simon Wolf, for example, is mentioned many times as a participant in the activities of various German societies in Washington in the 1860s and later. He was often listed as a speaker at German fraternal functions and served on several boards.[21]

Jews also were identified with the Masonic order from the very beginning of the Washington Jewish community. We find Leopold Oppenheimer and S. N. Solomon initiated in 1853, Levi Cohen and Isaac Herzberg affiliating in 1857. A total of twenty-five men in the community joined the Masonic order between 1853 and 1865. All are listed in the Comprehensive Cemetery List. In addition to those mentioned above, these were: Adajah and Michael Behrend, Augustus Binswanger, J. H. and Mark Cohen, Bernard Gusdorf, A. A. Gutman, Abraham and Jacob Herman, Benjamin and Jonas Kaufman, Harry and Serf Levy, Henry Strasberg, Henry Moses, S. J. and Solomon Strauss, Simon and William Wolf, and Max Weyl.[22]

We are unable to find records of Jews holding offices in the local Masonic order. The 1860 *Boyd's Directory*, however, lists Morris Adler as Secretary to Potomac Lodge No. 5. From conversations with several Masonic leaders in Washington, the author concludes that Jewish interest in Masonry is explained by the liberal tenets of the order, the ready acceptance of Jews into membership, and the leadership of Jews in the establishment of Masonry in America.

Notices of cultural activities appeared in 1863 in two leading Jewish periodicals. One traveling editor wrote:

> Another institution…is the "Washington Literary and Dramatic Association," comprising coreligionists exclusively, and boasting now of seventy-five members. A course of lectures was announced to be delivered before them by the following gentlemen: Park Benjamin; Henry Ward Beecher; Horace Greeley; John W. Forney; Mr. West, Editor of the *Chronicle*;
>
> Mr. Max Cohnheim, Editor of the *Columbia*; Raphael J. De Cordova; and Dr. Isaac M. Wise. A more ambitious undertaking than any of our metropolitan societies, however pretentious, have as yet attempted.
>
> They had just commenced a library, which already embraced three hundred volumes. It was surprising to see the interest displayed by the members, almost all of whom are engaged in mercantile pursuits. Meetings are held every Sunday afternoon.
>
> Great credit is due to the officers, among whom are recognized several New Yorkers; Captain Isaac Gotthold, formerly of this city, is President; Joseph H. Manheimer, Treasurer; A. Binswanger, Secretary, and Messrs. Ellis Lyons, Marcus J. Waldheimer, Solomon A. Rider, and G. H. Lesser are the Curators.

The editor also mentioned that, besides this, there are two other societies among our co-religionists in Washington, Harmonie Circle and Select Assembly – these being social, rather than literary, organizations.[23]

In the fall of 1863, the Reverend Isaac Leeser, while visiting Washington, reported:

> a Literary Society is in full operation. A meeting was held on Sunday afternoon, August 2d, at which among others, Mr. Simon

> Wolf, a young lawyer, delivered a pleasing address, which he has printed for private circulation.[24]

Charitable functions on behalf of the synagogue were held occasionally in the nation's capital. Reverend Leeser reports on a ball in his news column:

> In the evening we were invited to attend a ball given in honor of the opening of the Synagogue, the proceeds of which were to be devoted in its behalf. We repaired to the Odd Fellows Hall, where the festivities took place, and, notwithstanding the great heat, there were assembled several hundred young Israelites, who filled the room to such an extent that all could not participate in the amusement at one time. We certainly had no idea that so many of our people could be brought together in Washington; but there they were, many the residents of the city, others of Alexandria and Baltimore, and some of New York.[25]

In 1864, the Reverend Isaac Leeser once again had occasion to visit Washington. He reported in glowing terms the activities of the local Jewish cultural group:

> There is another institution of Washington which is afforded me decided gratification to visit and revisit; the headquarters of the Literary and Dramatic Association. The members of this young Society have developed more enterprise than any similar body of Jewish young men throughout the country.
>
> They have a commodious suite of rooms on Pennsylvania Avenue opposite the Metropolitan Hotel, – one apartment fitted up as a library and reading room, another arranged with tables for chess, checkers, dominoes (and no cards), and a third, of larger size, adapted for the purpose of a meeting room. They have given during the winter a series of soirees which were quite enjoyable. On the Sunday afternoon that I called at the rooms there were

> a number of gentlemen in the Library...Among them the Hon. Myer Strouse, Member of Congress from Pennsylvania.
>
> But of the Society – it now numbers about 75 members; Simon Wolf, Esq., of the Washington Bar, is President...Several gentlemen of the legal editorial professions adorn the rolls; but the preponderance of members represents the mercantile class.[26]

B'nai B'rith entered into the life of the Washington Jewish community early in 1864. This event was described as follows:

> On Sunday, January 31, the new lodge of B'nai B'rith, lately organized at the capital under the name Elijah Lodge No. 50, was duly installed by a delegation of the Grand Lodge No. 3, consisting of Raphael Teller, Lewis Ellinger, Sol Hoffheimer, Isaac Leeser, and B. Burgauer, besides whom were president G. Vasen of Philadelphia; I. Simson, M. H. Weil, and – Gusdorf, of Baltimore. G. Siegel was elected President. After the installation, the delegates were entertained by a supper at the house of Mr. Beggardt. The new society consists of about twenty-eight members.[27]

The next year Leeser again reported on the local B'nai B'rith on the occasion of his addressing Elijah Lodge.[28] He was gratified to learn that in fourteen months it had done much good and acquired capital of over $900. He noted that good will and order prevailed among the members. He was again asked to speak to the lodge (in German) on "the tendency and object of the order."

The Harmonie Club, mentioned earlier, comes in for further public notice. Simon Wolf reports that "the Harmonie Club will on Purim, give a 'Mask Ball' which promises to be a success."[29] In the same account the Reverend Leeser once again spoke of his invitation to address the Literary and Dramatic Association. In his speech he made the point that in the absence of high schools, such a society, where intellectual enjoyment is encouraged, is absolutely needed to withdraw young people from the card table and kindred pursuits.

Wolf reports further that the Association gave two public soirées at their hall that were well attended. He mentions that L. F. Tasitro, Esq., a well-known reader and elocutionist, gave a lecture on "The Stars That Have Set," which abounded in masterly delineations of character, eloquent and chaste, and was a decided and intellectual treat. On Washington's birthday a select soirée, held at Odd Fellows Hall, was graced by the wit and beauty of the Capital. *The Chronicle*, says Wolf, called it "the affair of the season."[30] On the 26th of February, Max Cohnheim, Esq., gave a humorous and musical soirée, assisted by some of the first talent of the city. At each of the soirées the members gave evidence, says Wolf, of their talent in recitations, music, song reading, poems and essays, and have established a character that would do Gotham no dishonor.[31]

The first Jewish religious school in the District of Columbia was opened in 1861 under the auspices of the Washington Hebrew Congregation.[32] This new congregation, in creating this day school, was following a pattern already set in many other cities.

Several factors influenced this small community to take this important step. First was the fact that the existing public school system was very inadequate in terms of building facilities and qualified teaching staff. Second was the fact that most of the Jews of Washington were recent arrivals from Germany. These parents wanted their children to study German as a means of preserving a connecting link with the home and culture left behind. German, an important subject in the new school's curriculum, was not offered by the public schools. Finally, more religious instruction could be imparted in a regular day school than in an afternoon or weekend school.

The Washington Hebrew Elementary School met daily from 9 to noon, and from 1 to 4 p.m. The morning was devoted to the study of Hebrew and German, and the afternoon to the teaching of English and kindred subjects. Members of the congregation paid a dollar a month tuition, and non-members a dollar and a half for each child. In 1865, the only year for which any figures are available, there were seventy-five children in the school; sixty-four of members and eleven of non-members. Dr. Henry Hochheimer of Baltimore came to Washington to examine classes every three months.

The Reverend S. Weil, who served the congregation from 1860 through 1867, was the school's first teacher, holding this position through the Civil War period.[33] From 1861 to 1863 the school met in rented quarters. In the latter year the Congregation purchased a church building on 8th Street for a permanent synagogue and school. Here the school continued to meet through the entire Civil War period.

III. ECONOMIC STATUS

A few Jewish merchants, attracted by the business prospects of Washington, settled in the early 1850s. More came in the latter part of the decade, almost all recent arrivals from the German states and principalities.

On the eve of the outbreak of the Civil War, Washington, including the prosperous port of Georgetown, had a population of 75,000. It had experienced a steady growth, stimulated by the growing immigration from Europe and its increasing importance as the nation's capital. In 1840, its population was 44,000; by 1850, it had reached almost 52,000. In the next decade, despite the retrocession of thirty square miles of territory, including Alexandria, to Virginia, the population increased almost fifty per cent.[34]

The economic life of Washington depended largely upon the fact that it was the nation's capital. The people earned their livelihoods mainly in providing the goods and services needed by the thousands of workers in the executive and legislative branches of the federal government and the additional numbers who came to the seat of government on business. Georgetown, a separate city although part of the District of Columbia, had a number of mills and factories and a certain amount of shipping trade that helped to support its population.

More than fifty Jewish families appear on the 1860 census enumerators' sheets for the District of Columbia.[35] This identification was made on the basis of similar names appearing on both the enumerators' sheets and on the consolidated cemetery list. An analysis of the data reveals a median age of twenty-six for all adult males and a median age of twenty-five for all adult females. Among the fifty-six employed persons in this group, forty-one were born in the German states, nine in the United States, and five in other European countries (Poland, Austria, and England). All four employed Jewish women were milliners.

Among the fifty-one employed men, the distribution of occupations was as follows:

OCCUPATION	NUMBER
Merchants	29
Clerks (chiefly in stores)	9
Watch repair and jewelry	2
Shoemaker	2
Pawnbroker	2
Cigar manufacturer	1
Surgeon	1
Lawyer	1
Engineer	1
Teacher	1
Laborer	1
Clergyman	1
TOTAL	51

Thus we have a picture in 1860 of the Jewish community forming an insignificant segment of the total population, fewer than 200 out of 75,000. Counting "clerks" and those providing services such as shoemakers and watch repairmen, we find that eighty-eight per cent were in some mercantile field.

The economic picture began to change drastically after the outbreak of war. Freight yards, hotels, restaurants, and barrooms carried on a rushing business. Soldiers were everywhere. The price of foodstuffs soared.[36] The city enjoyed a new material prosperity as the war went on. Commissary and quartermaster supplies poured into the city month after month. New warehouses went up and the government bought, leased, or built offices, hospitals, and workshops for the repair of military equipment. Twenty-five military hospitals came into existence in the Washington area.[37]

The demand for food, lodging, household goods, and clothes sent prices skyrocketing. The war was enriching tailors, merchants, blacksmiths, saddlers, and food purveyors. There were now some 450 restaurants and bars. Liquor license fees jumped from a pre-war $10,000 average to $91,000 in 1863.[38] According to a contemporary newspaper, army contractors, men seeking special favors, and heavy-hearted men and women who came to inquire for wounded relatives filled the hotels to overflowing. Five hundred new arrivals a day came to be commonplace.[39]

Business increased by leaps and bounds with the growth in population, increase in transients, and the influx of tens of thousands of soldiers who were assigned to guard the capital or were en route to the scene of conflict in the South. These, then, were the economic circumstances that attracted many new businessmen, Jews and non-Jews alike, to the nation's capital during the war years. Significant changes occurred in the Jewish community after the outbreak of war.

By 1862, the influx of Jewish newcomers was considerable. A "Correspondent" reports that:

> The number of Israelites quartered in Washington and its vicinity (exclusive of those in the Army) cannot fall short of two thousand. As evidence of their presence, there are at least half a dozen kosher restaurants, all of which appear to flourish to the satisfaction of their proprietors. At one of them in particular, about dinner hour, there were forty guests seated at the same time, and, on their departure, an equal number ready to take their places. Many are the commercial establishments conducted under names familiar to a New Yorker. All departments of trade seem to be favored with a full representation from the metropolitan district.[40]

In Boyd's *Directory* for 1862, we find many advertisements of Jewish firms. Wertheimer and Company, were "Importers and Dealers in Brandies, Wines and Segars – Officers and Sutlers Supplied." C. Hammerschlag carried a large notice of his "Most Extensive Pie and Cake Bakery in Washington City." Among brokers was listed Henry Levy.

By 1863, when assessments were made in connection with the wartime income tax, we are able to identify 114 Jewish names in the records.[41] This was done, as before, by a comparison of these names with names on our Consolidated Cemetery List. There were no doubt many more. Among these 114 Jewish businessmen, seventy per cent were classified as peddlers who sold their wares to sick and wounded soldiers in the hospitals or to visitors in the city. Another four per cent were hotel or innkeepers, and six per cent each were in manufacturing and wholesaling. Thus, in a short space of three years we find Jews in several new areas of business.

The manuscript reports of Dun and Bradstreet shed added light on the status of Jewish businessmen during the Civil War.[42] These reports typically present them as small operators who are doing well and have a good, though limited, credit rating. The four cases cited are identified as Jewish, from the Consolidated Cemetery list:

> Louis Barr is reported (June, 1865) as "making money and has accumulated considerable since the war commenced... worth $2,000 to $5,000..."
>
> A. Kaufman (May, 1864) is considered good for small bills... fair stock and business.
>
> Bernard Silverberg (June, 1864)...has been a bookkeeper, and now takes the fancy dry good store formerly kept by Mrs. John D. Evans...In July, they report: Probably has $3,000 to $4,000 capacity...young married man of good habits and fair prospects.
>
> Max Weyl, later a famous artist, is reported (November, 1861): Small means, hardly more than watch repairer...entitled to only small credit...The epilogue (October, 1877) states: Out of business...wife doing small business...has a stock of $800 or $900....

Mr. Weyl, a business failure, was encouraged to take up art by the painter Samuel H. Kaufmann, President of Board of Directors of the Corcoran Gallery of Art, who taught him free of charge. He subsequently achieved fame as an artist, winning many prizes and medals. His works are in the permanent collections of the National Gallery of Art and the Corcoran Gallery of Art.[43]

Simon Wolf reports on the general economic status of Washington's Jewry as follows:

> It is my pleasant duty to record a favorable change in the condition of the Jewish residents in the capital of the nation... Previous to the war, there were but few of our People living here, and their *status* was not everything that could be desired; but now, their number is largely in excess of the percentage of increase of the entire population, and they are to be found... successfully competing with their fellow citizens in Commerce, in the Arts, at the Bar, and in the Halls of Legislation.[44]

One of the outstanding businesses in Washington during the Civil War period was that of Philp and Solomons, booksellers, printers, and publishers. A visitor reports:

> Mr. Adolphus Solomons (of Philp and Solomons) whose place of business in Pennsylvania Avenue is the resort of men of letters (for whose accommodations they have a costly "study" attached to their store) extended us the hospitalities of his house; and we passed a pleasant Sabbath with him and his good family. We were pleased to find Mr. S. doing so well in the capital, especially as he is one of the very few Israelites there who observe the Sabbath.[45]

No information is available that would identify Franklin Philp, Solomon's partner, as a Jew. Philp's name first appears in the *City Directory* in 1858, listed as a salesman. His name appears in every subsequent directory until 1875. Beginning in 1860, he is shown as Solomons's partner, and in 1875, he is listed alone as a bookseller, at 909 Pennsylvania Avenue. By this time, Solomons had left Washington for New York City. Philp probably was a bachelor since he is listed as rooming at six different addresses in city directories between 1858 and 1875.

This firm also made its contribution to the appreciation of fine arts. A local directory informs us that "Washington artists frequently exhibit their works in the gallery belonging to Philp and Solomons."[46] Later we find this news item of interest:

> There are one or two points in and about Washington where you are pretty certain to happen upon "notabilities," there is Philp and Solomons'[s] bookstore on the Avenue...its shelves presenting a tempting array of the newest and best issues from the press....[47]

In a later issue, under the heading of "The Fine Arts" we are informed that:

> Messrs. Philp and Solomons are the publishers of all photographs produced at this establishment (Gardner Photographic Gallery) as well as The Metropolitan Gallery on Pennsylvania Avenue, and will shortly issue a handsome volume entitled *Gardner's Photographic Sketches of the War* in a style of magnificence worthy of the subject.[48]

The following advertisements of books issued by Philps and Solomons are indicative of their publishing activities:

> NEW PUBLICATIONS
>
> Army and Navy Almanac and Washington Military Directory for the year 1863; containing, in addition to a calendar and the ordinary almanac information, tables of reference on matters of special interest to the united services – Edited by Ben. Perley Poore – Washington. *Philp & Solomons, 1863.*
>
> ————————
>
> Regulations for the Field Service of Cavalry in Time of War. by George B. McClellan, Major-General, U.S. Army – Fully illustrated. Washington, D.C. Philp & Solomons, Publishers and Army Stationers, 1863.[49]

This firm was a major supplier of stationery and related items to the House of Representatives during the latter part of the Civil War period. The annual report of the Clerk of the House reveals an expenditure of almost $33,000 to four stationers; of that, Philp and Solomons accounts for $26,102, or almost eighty per cent of the total.[50] During 1864, this firm received twenty orders for a very wide variety of merchandise. The bulk was for paper goods of every description, but many unusual items were supplied. One order, in the amount of $50, was for a large framed photograph of the Speaker of the House. Another expensive requisition was for a quantity of porte-monnaies, in velvet, leather, and pearl. These were purses or wallets, fashionable at the time.

This firm was also asked to supply, often in gross or thousand quantity, such items as ivory folders, pocket knives, diaries, autograph books, quill pens, pen cutters, and sand boxes [ash trays?]. Among luxury items were enameled gold cases, agate seals, gloss inkstands and gold mounted, screw-propelling pencils – forerunners of our present day mechanical pencil. Another item, which we are unable to identify, was the "ne plus ultra" of which 50 gross were ordered at one time. Could this have been a paper clip or straight pin? The item purchased in huge quantity in 1864 was speech envelopes. These were used by Members of Congress to mail their two-to-twenty page speeches to constituents. Six orders, totaling 5,160,000 envelopes, were filled by this firm. One million of these were designated "extra heavy" to accommodate the bulkier speeches of long-winded orators.

It is evident from this sampling of services rendered to one chamber of the legislative branch of government for one year, that the firm of Philp and Solomons played an important role in supplying the United States Government with one of the sinews of war, the paper goods needed to record the activities of government.

The local Jewish community was too small to support a newspaper of its own. However, members of the community supported the local German weekly newspaper. In 1863, Max Cohnheim, a Jewish journalist from New York, established a German language weekly, *Columbia*, in Washington. Cohnheim had taken an active part in the German Revolution of 1848, was indicted for high treason in Baden in 1848, and sentenced to eight years in prison. He succeeded in escaping and fled to the United States.

In New York he became a successful author and composed many farces and dramas in the 1850s.[51] He wrote one of the first plays directed specifically for the German-American stage, *Herz und Dollar.* Another of his propaganda plays, *Fursten zum Land Hinaus*, portrayed the final triumph of republicanism in Germany.[52] Cohnheim established a magazine, *The New York Humorist,* which flourished from 1858 until 1861. He then left for Washington where he obtained a position with the Treasury Department. Secure in his new job, he sought an outlet for his journalistic interests. He found a printer in Werner Koch. Financial support came from Nicholas Weygand, a wine and liquor dealer, and Ferdinand Kasche, a prosperous hotel owner.

Cohnheim's new weekly made its first appearance on October 17, 1863. Beginning with 200 subscribers, the list climbed to 800 within four months and exceeded 1,600 for 1865.[53] Cohnheim enthusiastically supported the Lincoln administration during the three and one-half years he edited this newspaper. His news columns were almost entirely oriented to national political and cultural matters. He devoted space liberally to local German cultural events and to war news of local interest.

The two great issues concerning Jews – the chaplaincy and the notorious General Orders No. 11 – occurred before *Columbia* entered the scene. The only reference to Jewish matters are announcements of local events. The issue of December 5, 1863 [p. 5] announced the Washington Literary and Dramatic Society's First Series of Literary Events. Dr. Isaac M. Wise lectured on "The Jewish People – Their History" and R. J. DeCordova, a popular lecturer of the day, spoke on "Life and Liberty." The issue of December 12 [p. 5], carried further note of Dr. Wise's lecture, and identified him as editor of *The Israelite*. The following week's issue [p. 5] informed readers that Dr. Wise would speak at the Synagogue on Saturday in German, and on Sunday in English. The German Aid Society for Sick and Wounded Soldiers, of which G. Cohen was Corresponding Secretary, was publicized in several issues of *Columbia* beginning on January 9, 1864. This Society sponsored a Great Fair, and sought the support of the entire German community. The May 14 issue of *Columbia* [p. 3] carried a prominently placed story on the retirement of Isaac Gotthold as president of the Washington Literary and Dramatic Society. Included was a lengthy resolution recounting his services to the organization.

In his editorials, Cohnheim attacked everything that seemed conventional, and often he directed his editorial barbs against all religious sects. *Columbia* became the most colorful German language paper ever published in Washington. Occasionally he opened his columns to those whom he attacked.

In the issue following Lincoln's death, all pages of *Columbia* were bordered in black to express the profound sorrow of German-Americans everywhere. On August 14, 1865, *Columbia* appealed to German societies in the city to help raise funds for a Lincoln statue. Many public events took place to raise a substantial sum, which was used in 1868 to erect a statue to Lincoln in front of City Hall.

With business booming during the war years, Cohnheim found ready support for his weekly through advertisements by the businessmen of German origin, both Jewish and Christian. We find advertisements of the following Jewish business houses: Wolf and Hart, Julius Loewenthal, Levi Baar, L. Seldner, Gotthelf and Behrend, Lansburgh and Bro., Philp and Solomons, J. Biggardt and Joseph Nathan. These names are identified with the Jewish community of the 1860s.

Cohnheim was so encouraged by this success that he resigned his government position on April 1, 1866, and moved his office from Koch's print shop to a more commodious location on Pennsylvania Avenue. These steps were taken almost at the start of a post-war business recession that saw large numbers of German-Americans leave Washington. *Columbia's* revenues fell sharply while expenses remained at a new high level.

On January 12, 1867, Cohnheim had to inform his readers that "family reasons force us to resign." Heavily in debt, Cohnheim suddenly departed for San Francisco and was never again seen in the District of Columbia. Werner Koch took over publication of *Columbia*, continuing as editor-publisher until March 1873, when his paper was merged with the *Journal.* After the Civil War, Nehemiah H. Miller began publication of a daily, the *Täglicher Washingtoner Anzeiger.* L. Kronheimer was a frequent contributor to the German language *Washington Journal.*[54]

The city directories of the war years reveal the influx of several Jewish professionals. Hutchinson's *Washington and Georgetown Directory* for 1863 lists a physician, Phineas J. Horwitz, and Simon Wolf, a lawyer.

Dr. Jonathan P. Horwitz, born in Baltimore in 1822, received his medical training at Jefferson Medical College in Philadelphia. He entered the U.S. Navy as Assistant Surgeon in 1847. From 1859 until 1865 he was a medical officer in the Bureau of Medicine and Surgery, in Washington, D.C., and was promoted to Chief of the Bureau in 1865, serving in that capacity until July 1, 1869.[55]

Dr. Adajah Behrend, who received his medical degree from Georgetown University, was born in Hanover, Germany in 1841. He entered the Union Army as a private, transferred to the 2nd U.S. Regulars, and was promoted to Hospital Steward with the Army of the Potomac, in Washington. He was wounded by gunfire near Harrisons' Landing on the James River, and invalided home. For a time he served as demonstrator of anatomy at his alma mater. He served as Physician to the Poor in the Fourth Ward of Washington.[56]

Boyd's *Washington and Georgetown Directory* for 1865 lists Simon Wolf and Abraham Hart as lawyers; Julius Loewenthal and Co., as "attorneys for prosecution of claims before all departments and Court of Claims"; and an additional physician, Leonard Baum. The firm of Gritzer and Cohen is listed under patent agents. In the same directory we find the list of a number of Jewish-owned or operated boarding houses and hotels. Isaac Beggardt [Biggardt], Myer May, and Alois Kohn are the boarding house operators, while William Rothschild ran the Admiral House and William Hochherz the Clinton Hotel.

The following advertisement appeared in *The Occident* on several occasions during the war period:

> **כשר**
>
> BOARDING HOUSE AT WASHINGTON, D.C.
>
> No. 366 C Street, between 4-1/2 and 6th Streets
> The subscriber takes this method of informing the public that he has lately taken the above establishment, formerly kept by Mr. J. Hildensheim, and will endeavor to do all in his power to render customers' stays agreeable while at his house, which is within a few minutes walk of the capitol, and in a pleasant part of the city.[57]

From the scattered evidence reported here, it is apparent that a considerable number of Jewish businessmen, individuals with varied experience and backgrounds, were attracted to Washington after the outbreak of the Civil War. For the most part this was a highly transient population, men coming and going with the changing fortunes of business and with the fluctuations in the political and military situation between 1861 and 1865. The transitory nature of this group is evident from the absence of a great many of them from congregational membership rosters, and from the changes in listings and advertisements in city directories during the war years.

IV. SERVICE IN THE UNION CAUSE

The Jewish community in the nation's capital shared the pro-Union sentiments that prevailed in Washington after 1861. These feelings were strengthened as the war dragged on with its suffering and deaths of hundreds of thousands. Havoc struck Washington with particular force because of its proximity to the seat of war, and its twenty-odd military hospitals, which cared for a multitude of sick and wounded. Washington's small Jewish community shared with their fellow citizens the humanitarian impulse to give succor to these war sufferers. They gave generously of their time and money, both as individuals and through their congregation.

Walt Whitman noted that, at times, 50,000 men lay in the military hospitals in the Washington area, "a population more numerous in itself than the Washington of ten or fifteen years ago." Wounded men filled improvised wards in churches, in the Insane Asylum, in the halls of the Capitol and at the Patent Office.[58]

Simon Wolf, as spokesman for the Jewish community, proposed a Jewish military hospital for the capital:

> Every Israelite must be proud at the readiness displayed by our co-religionists in responding to the call of their country, for its protection. Everywhere...they have come nobly forth amongst the very first to offer, upon the altar of the sacred Union, their might, their intellect, their treasure, and, if need be, their very heart's blood. ...
>
> Let us not forget to care for him when his manly form is stricken with disease, or he lays wounded on the battlefield. I am led to these remarks from having had an excellent opportunity to observe the manner the sick are treated in the Hospitals and Infirmary in this place, all of which fall far short of what they should be...A hospital for our people is what we want here.[59]
>
> ...It has been my privilege to pass time among these co-religionists (sick and wounded) both among our own troops and among the rebel prisoners in hospitals, and if my pen enabled me to convey to the reader one tithe of what I have witnessed, I am sure this feeble appeal for assistance will be responded to with a will and alacrity worthy of the well-known instincts of our people and the cause of our common country.[60]

Despite Wolf's advocacy and editorial support from the Jewish press, a "Jews Hospital for Soldiers" never saw the light of day. Capt. Jonas M. Levy, another spokesman for the local Jewish community, also appealed for aid to stricken Jewish soldiers. He strongly urged "to again call the attention of our readers to the necessity of providing for the wants of Jewish soldiers in the hospitals in and around the capital."[61]

The absence of a nurse corps in the Union Army in the early years of the war led to creation of a body of volunteer nurses, made up of women connected with religious congregations. The late Mrs. Theresa Taussig, whose father,

Leopold Karpeles,[62] served in the Civil War and later took up residence in Washington, D.C., describes the war service of the women of Washington Hebrew Congregation as told to her by her father:

> As in all wards the ladies of Washington aided the overtaxed hospital personnel in caring for the wounded. The daughters of my late grandparents, the Rev. Simon and Hannah Mundheim, were among these good Samaritans.[63]

This statement is corroborated in part by an official medical record on Karpeles in which mention is made of Miss Sara Mundheim as being his nearest relative, whom he subsequently married. A correspondent identified as "M" corroborates Mrs. Taussig's statement regarding hospital services of the local community:

> The congregation deserves the acknowledgements of American Israelites for the care and attention they have paid to Jewish soldiers, ill and dying, in the department of Washington. They have looked after the interment of many co-religionists who had no other claim upon them than that of brotherhood.[64]

Simon Wolf reported on another aspect of the Jewish community's war services:

> In the report just published of the Fair lately held here in aid of the Sanitary Commission, I observe that the Hebrew Society's table is credited for $756.95; and when I tell you the entire receipts were only $10,661.47, you will readily perceive how large a proportion of the amount realized is due to the Hebrew congregation. The ladies had the matter in charge and were beaten by only one other table, that of the Treasury Department. All honor to our fair Jewesses![65]

Toward the close of the war, at a time when thousands of wounded and sick soldiers were still in hospitals, and maimed veterans were becoming a common sight in almost every community, Nathan Grossmayer, a Washington merchant, was moved to write a letter to the President. His letter follows:

> Washington, D.C.
> November 16th, 1864
>
> To His Ex. Abraham Lincoln
> President of the Unites States
>
> Dear Sir:
>
> As an adopted citizen of the United States I permit myself to make a few suggestions for the welfare of our wounded patriotic soldiers, wounded to such a degree that it is impossible for them to make a living in any way and are obliged to beg their bread from house to house.
>
> I have seen in Paris that the soldiers wounded to such a degree are the pride of the country and there is the splendid house "Les Invalides" where they are taken care of to the honor of the country; why should we in a land so blessed in every way, do less for our patriots than the Governments of Europe. Therefore, I propose that such a place be provided by patriotic subscribers and the place well adapted for it would be the Central Park in New York City. The City no doubt would be proud of giving such a ground for such a noble purpose.
>
> If such idea would meet with your view although I am not rich I would open the Subscription with One Thousand Dollars.
>
> Hoping to be honored with a reply
> I am very respectfully
> Your obt. Servant
>
> Nathan Grossmayer
> 274 Penn Avenue
> Washington, D.C.[66]

Lincoln was assassinated before he was able to act on Grossmayer's suggestions. The latter repeated his proposal in a letter to President Andrew Johnson, enclosing his contribution of $1,000, and suggesting that the home he designated as a memorial to Lincoln.[67]

Public interest in providing for sick and disabled veterans, as exemplified by Grossmayer's proposal, led to prompt action by Congress. On March 3, 1865, Congress passed a law providing for the establishment of asylums,

> for the officers and men of the volunteer forces of the United States, totally disabled by wounds received or sickness contracted while in the line of their duty during the present Rebellion.

This law was liberalized by an amendatory act passed March 21, 1866.[68] The National Military and Naval Asylum, the title of our first soldiers' home, was incorporated in 1866. The central asylum was located at Dayton, Ohio, and it was followed by the creation of a number of branches in various sections of the country.[69]

Several Jewish men who served during the Civil War, and who were not previous residents of Washington, settled in the nation's capital at the end of the war where they made noteworthy contributions to the life of the community.

Moses Bruckheimer came to this country in 1860, enlisted in the 66th N.Y. Infantry in April, 1861. Discharged for disability near the end of the war, he entered Columbia University, receiving his M.D. degree in 1868. He married Henrietta Fuchs and established a medical practice in Washington, where he remained until his death in 1903.[70]

Bernard Nordlinger enlisted in the "German Artillery" of Macon, Georgia, serving as a bugler in Beauregard's Division. He was later promoted to sergeant, and was wounded at the Second Battle of Bull Run. He settled in the District immediately after the close of the war, becoming a merchant in Georgetown.[71]

Charles Stein, whose real name was George Stern, enlisted in the U.S. Marine Corps in June 1864 in Philadelphia. He was promoted to sergeant and later was captured by the Confederates. He was imprisoned in Pensacola and freed near the close of the war. He, too, settled in Washington and opened a butcher shop.[72]

We know of thirty-three Jewish men in Washington who heeded the call to the colors for defense of the Union. This is a large number, considering the size of the Jewish community and the fact that many were recent arrivals in the United States. The District of Columbia Civil War Index at the National Archives contains over 16,000 names. From the list, well over 100 were extracted for further study through checking of military and pension files and a later checking with the consolidated cemetery list of the three oldest congregations in the city. The following list names soldiers, taken from the Index, and identified as Jewish from the cemetery list.

An asterisk indicates that the name appears on the Consolidated Cemetery List of the Jewish Historical Society of Greater Washington. An "f" signified that this family name appears in the cemetery list.

The Jewish community, like other groups in the nation's capital, was profoundly affected by the assassination of Lincoln. They shared the public grief at the loss of their noble president. In the newspaper accounts of the events following Lincoln's death we find references to the participation of the Jewish community.

On April 19th, there was a notice of a "Meeting of German Citizens."

> At a large meeting of German citizens of the city, held at the Winter Garden, of which Mr. Cohnheim, Editor of *Columbia* was president, the following resolutions were unanimously adopted....

The following day, under "Order of Procession" for Lincoln's funeral, "German Societies" were among those listed. In the same column is listed "The Hebrew Congregation, one hundred and twenty-five men, marshaled by Benjamin Kaufman."[73]

NAME		COMPANY	BATTALION
Adajah Behrend		Degges	2nd U.S. Regulars
Jacob N. Cohn	f	Degges	5th
Jacob P. Fass	f	L	1st D C Cav.
*Jacob Fisher			1st D C Cav.
Chas. Freirick		B	8th
George Freund	f	J	2nd Inf.
*Michael Freund		J	2nd Inf.
Henry Gerber	f	E	6th Inf.
Joseph Goldsmith	f	Boyd's	1st D C Cav.
*Henry Haas		B	8th
*William Hahn		A	8th
Seigfriend Hammerschlag	f	Degges	5th D C Cav.
*Michael Hoffa		A	8th
David Jacob	f	C-	8th
Almond Jacobs	f	H	1st
Daniel King	f	--	--
*Henry King		--	--
Moses King	f	--	--
*Samuel King		--	--
Adolph Lowenthal	f	E	2nd
Samuel Marks	f	--	--
*Louis Mundheim		A	8th
*Abraham Rosenthal		A	1st
Jacob A. Schloss	f	A	1st
Adolphus Schwab	f	A	1st
Joshua Sinsheimer	f	I and A	1st
Joseph Solomon	f	C	2nd
*Julius Stein		A	8th
William Stein	f	I	2nd
Richard Steinberg	f	A	1st
Henry Steiner	f	D	2nd
George Stern		--	--
Louis Witkowsky	f	C	1st

The following day, we find a news account entitled, "Proposed Monument to President Lincoln":

> A movement is about to be inaugurated in this city looking to the erection of a monument to the memory of President Lincoln. An offer has already been made, Messrs. Lansburgh & Bro. agreeing to head the list with $500.00. They will at once hand this amount over to any individual or organization who may be authorized to receive it for the purpose indicated.[74]

Newspapers carried descriptions of the manner in which businesses exhibited their sorrow at Lincoln's death. "At the store of Philp and Solomons, the right window contained a colored portrait of the President and his son Tad. This was the last sitting of Mr. Lincoln for a picture. Both windows were heavily draped with white and black cambric. The balcony was heavily draped and in white letters on black background appeared these words: 'Treason Has Done His Worst.'"[75]

CONCLUSION

During the critical war years the Washington Jewish community was but a tiny minority, hardly more than one per cent of the total population of the nation's capital. They were largely of German origin, having arrived in the United States within a decade or at most fifteen years prior to the outbreak of the conflict.

The Jewish segment differed from the total resident population in the fact that virtually all of its members were in business, with a small proportion in the professions. The activities of the Literary Society, B'nai B'rith, and other social-cultural groups in the Jewish community strongly suggest that virtually all were literate.

Washington's Jews shared with their fellow citizens the prevailing beliefs, hopes, and attitudes toward the war and toward the basic issues of slavery and the preservation of the Union. The victories and the defeats of war affected them as much as it did their neighbors. Jews served with Christians in the many home-front welfare, nursing, and fundraising activities of the war years.

The number of Israelites increased considerably as the war progressed. Thousands of Northerners, Jews and non-Jews alike, were drawn to the nation's capital – the seat of government and the center of the war effort.

All of these war-related activities accelerated the Americanization of Washington's Jewry and helped to establish the community on a firmer basis. As Dr. Bertram W. Korn observed in his *American Jewry and the Civil War*, "In 1865 American Jewry was more than five years older (than in 1860); it had learned the lessons and gained the insights of several generations."

1 Identification of individuals as Jews was made from the consolidated cemetery list, 1860-1930, a project of the Jewish Historical Society of Greater Washington. This was prepared by the author with the cooperation of officers of Washington Hebrew Congregation, Adas Israel Congregation and Ohev Sholom Talmud Torah Congregation. The list includes additional names found in Nordlinger's *History of Washington Hebrew Congregation* and names found in *The Occident* and in *The Jewish Messenger.*

2 Louis Stern, "History of Washington Hebrew Congregation," published in *The Temple*, Washington, D.C., March, 1898, p.1, and republished in the *Washington Post*, July 13, 1901.

3 Bernard I. Nordlinger, *History of Washington Hebrew Congregation* (Washington, 1956), p. 11.
4 *The Occident* [=*Occ.*], vol. XIV, no. 1 (April, 1856), p. 41.
5 *Ibid.*
6 In Archives Room, Washington Hebrew Congregation.
7 *National Intelligencer* (Washington, D.C.), May 23, 1859.
8 *Occ.*, vol. XVIII, no. 32 (Nov., 1860), p. 195.
9 B. I. Nordlinger, *op. cit.*, p. 17.
10 *Occ.*, vol. XXI, no. 6 (Sept., 1863), pp. 273-274.
11 B. I. Nordlinger, *op. cit.*, p. 14.
12 *Occ.*, vol. XXI, no. 3 (June, 1863), p. 32.
13 *Occ.*, vol. XXI, no. 6 (Sept., 1863), pp. 273-274.
14 *Evening Star* (Washington, D.C.), Aug. 1, 1863.
15 Minutes, Washington Hebrew Congregation, Sept. 8, 1867 and Oct. 13, 1867.
16 *Jewish Messenger* [=*JM*], vol. XIV, no. 22 (Dec. 11, 1863).
17 *JM*, vol. XV, no. 17 (May 6, 1864), p. 134.
18 *Occ.*, vol. XXIII, no. 5 (May, 1865), p. 95.
19 *Ibid.*
20 *Occ.*, vol. XV, no. 9 (Dec., 1857), p. 424.
21 Society for History of Germans in Maryland, *Thirtieth Report* (Baltimore, 1959), pp. 49-50.
22 Letter from the Secretary to author, Sept. 10, 1962, Records of the Grand Lodge, Free and Accepted Masons of the District of Columbia.
23 *JM*, vol. XIV, no. 22 (Dec. 11, 1863), p. 200.
24 *Occ.*, vol. XXI, no. 6 (Sept., 1863), p. 274.
25 *Ibid.*
26 *JM*, vol. XV, no. 8 (Feb. 26, 1864), p. 59.
27 *Occ.*, vol. XXI, no. 12 (March, 1864), p. 568.
28 *Occ.*, vol. XXIII, no. 2 (May, 1856), p. 95.
29 *JM*, vol. XVII, no. 11 (March 17, 1865), p. 96.
30 *Occ.*, vol. XXIII, no. 2 (May, 1865), p. 95.
31 *JM*, vol. XVIII, no. 11 (March 17, 1865), p. 96.
32 Nathan M. Kaganoff, "The Education of the Jewish Child in the District of Columbia, 1861-1915," American University, Master's Thesis, 1956, pp. 1-5.
33 Abram Simon, *A History of Washington Hebrew Congregation* (Washington, 1905), p. 21.
34 Federal Writers Project, W.P.A., *Washington City and Capital* (Washington, D.C., 1937), p. 54.
35 Decennial Census of 1860, District of Columbia, National Archives.
36 *Evening Star* (Washington, D.C.), April 22, 23, May 14, and July 2, 1861.
37 Constance M. Green, *Washington Village and Capital, 1800-1878* (Princeton, 1962), p. 262.
38 *Evening Star*, Feb. 6 and May 2, 1862; April 4 and Sept. 14, 1863.
39 *The Chronicle* (Washington, D.C.), Aug. 5 and Sept. 7, 1863.
40 *JM*, vo. XI, no. 3 (Jan. 24, 1862), p. 28.
41 Assessment Records Books, Washington, D.C., 1863. Fiscal Records Branch, National Archives.

42 Dun and Bradstreet, Reports, vol. IV, District of Columbia,
Archives of Harvard School of Business Administration, Cambridge, Mass.
43 *Dictionary of American Painters, Sculptors and Engravers* (New York, 1965),
edited by Mantle Fielding, pp. 402 and 525.
44 *JM*, vol. XV, no. 17 (May 6, 1864), p. 134.
45 *JM*, vol. XI, no. 3 (Jan. 24, 1862), p. 24.
46 *Philps' Washington Described* (Washington, D.C., 1860),
edited by William D. Haley, p. 216.
47 *JM*, vol. XV, no. 8 (Feb. 26, 1864), p. 59.
48 *JM*, vol. XVI, no. 22 (Dec. 9, 1864), p. 173.
49 *JM*, vol. XIII, no. 14 (April 3, 1863), p. 117.
50 *House of Representatives, 56th Congress, 2nd Session, Miscellaneous Documents, No. 29.*
"Contingent Expenses of the House of Representatives," Jan. 30, 1865.
51 Adolf Kober, "Jews in the Revolution of 1848 in Germany,"
Jewish Social Studies, vol. X, no. 2 (April, 1948), pp. 135-164.
52 Carl Wittke, *Refugees of Revolution* (Philadelphia, 1952), p. 288.
53 Klaus G. Wust, "German Immigrants and Their Newspapers in the
District of Columbia," Society for the History of Germans in Maryland,
Thirtieth Report (1959), p. 49.
54 *Ibid.*, p. 53.
55 *Dictionary of American Medical Biography*, edited by H. A. Kelly
(Philadelphia, 1928), p. 599.
56 Medical Society of the District of Columbia, *History, 1817-1909*, vol. I
(Washington, D.C., 1909), p. 280.
57 *Occ.*, vol. XXI, no. 7 (Oct., 1863), p. 316.
58 C.M. Green, *op. cit.*, p. 261.
59 *JM*, vol. IX, no. 21 (May 26, 1861), p. 165.
60 *JM*, vol. IX, no. 22 (June 7, 1861), p. 172.
61 *JM*, vol. XIII, no. 25 (June 26, 1863), p. 211.
62 *American Jewish Historical Quarterly*, vol. LII, no. 3 (March, 1963), p. 230.
63 Letter to author, July 23, 1959, deposited in B'nai B'rith Archives.
64 *JM*, vol. XV, no. 8 (Feb. 26, 1864), p. 59.
65 *JM*, vol. XV, no. 17 (May 6, 1864), p. 134.
66 Robert T. Lincoln Collection, No. 38395, Library of Congress.
67 Bertram W. Korn, *American Jewry and the Civil War* (Cleveland, 1961), p. 99.
68 National Home for Disabled Volunteer Soldiers, *Laws and Regulations*
(Washington, D.C., 1892), pp. 5-12.
69 *Ibid.*
70 Medical Society of the District of Columbia, *History*, p. 296.
71 Communication based on family records and history,
from Bernard I. Nordlinger, descendant.
72 *Ibid.*
73 *National Intelligencer* (Washington, D.C.), April 19-20, 1865.
74 *Ibid.*
75 *Evening Star*, April 20, 1865.

Acknowledgment of Exhibition Contributors

The following list recognizes the contributions that made the exhibition, Jewish Life in Mr. Lincoln's City, possible. We are grateful for this support, which was the basis for the creation of this book.

Curatorial Team
Laura Cohen Apelbaum, Executive Director
David McKenzie, Curatorial Associate
Wendy Turman, Curator/Archivist
Claire Uziel, Assistant Archivist
Marie Cohen
Nathalie Lavine

Exhibition Advisor
M. Ann Belkov

Script Writer
Sharon L. Barry

Curatorial Advisors
Dr. Pamela S. Nadell
Inaugural Patrick Clendenen
Professor of History and
Director of the Jewish Studies Program
American University

Dr. Marc Lee Raphael
Nathan Gumenick
Chair of Judaic Studies
College of William and Mary

Exhibition Design
The Design Minds, Inc.

This exhibition was made possible, in part, by the generous contributions of:

GENERALS
Robert H. Smith
Albert and Lillian Small Foundation
Small-Alper Family Foundation

MAJORS
Marshall B. Coyne Foundation
Brenda & Paul Pascal
Southern Jewish Historical Society
United Jewish Endowment
Fund of The Jewish Federation of Greater Washington

CAPTAINS
Abramson Family Foundation
Family of H. Max & Josephine F. Ammerman
Beth El Hebrew Congregation
Washington Hebrew Congregation
Martha & Stuart Bindeman
Family & Friends of Brenda Pascal

LIEUTENANTS
Laura & Perry Apelbaum
Peter Trooboff
Linda & James Cafritz
Maryann & Alvin Friedman
Steve Blacher

PRIVATES
Jane & David Fairweather Foundation
Judith & Michael Herman
Marky & Bo Kirsch
Marla Bobowick
Allen Berman
Phyllis & Sumner Myers

And many thanks to those who supported the creation of this exhibition with their time, knowledge, and expertise:

Diana Cohen Altman
Jennifer Hammond
Rabbi Brett Isserow, Beth El Hebrew Congregation
Cheryl Kempler
Rabbi Bruce Lustig, Washington Hebrew Congregation
Robert Marcus
Melissa Miller, Beth El Hebrew Congregation
Peggy Pearlstein
David Bruce Smith

JEWISH LIFE IN MR. LINCOLN'S CITY is designated an official program of the Lincoln Bicentennial Commission and Cultural Tourism DC's program, Living the Legacy: Lincoln in Washington, DC

THE JEWISH COMMUNITY IN WASHINGTON, D.C., DURING THE CIVIL WAR

Note: Washington has changed its street-numbering system, so the addresses listed are not the same as today's addresses.

NAME	AGE (1860)	OCCUPATION
Abraham, Levi	49	Merchant
Abraham, Elizabeth	18	
Abraham, Abraham	16	Clerk
Abraham, Samuel	14	
Abraham, Isaac	12	
Abraham, Jacob	8	
Abraham, Loman	4	
Abraham, Mark	3	
Adler, Adolph		Merchant
Adler, Henry	23	Merchant
Adler, Morris	62	Clerk
Adler, Morris J.	25	Merchant
Adler, Stella	18	Milliner
Alexander, Isaac	46	Jeweler
Barr, Berman	74	Retired
Barr, Isaac	26	Merchant
Barr, Levi	26	Merchant
Baum, Henry		
Baum, Leonard		Doctor
Baumgarten, Julius	40	Engraver
Behrend, Adajah	19	Hospital Steward
Behrend, Amnon	26	Merchant
Behrend, Sarah		
Behrend, Bendiza	33	Merchant
Behrend, Emma Pribram		Milliner
Behrend, Bernhard	67	
Behrend, Mathilda	18	
Behrend, Elon	31	Merchant
Behrend, Henrietta		
Benjamin, Judah P.	49	Senator
Biggardt, Isaac		Boarding House Owner
Binswanger, Augustus		Clothier
Berliner, Israel	16	Clerk
Berliner, Jonas	16	Clerk
Blout, Henry	27	Merchant
Boyer, John	30	Pawnbroker
Cohen, J.H.		Shoes
Cohen, Mark		
Cohen, Levi	38	Shoemaker
Cohen, Lena	33	
Cohen, Rachael	10	
Cohen, Mathilda	8	
Cohen, Fannie	5	
Cohen, Amelia	2	
Cohen, Morris	27	Clerk, Clothier
Cohenheim, Max		Editor
Colman, Henry	33	Merchant
Colman, Moses	24	Merchant
David, Abraham	27	Merchant
DeLeon, David C.	42	Surgeon
DeLeon, Edwin	38	Lawyer
DeLeon, Thomas C.	23	Civil Engineer

LACE OF BIRTH	HOME/BUSINESS LOCATION
oland	
oland	
oland	
oland	
ngland	
ew York	
ew York	
ew York	
ermany	Adler & Bro. Fancy Goods, 439 7th Street west (1860)
ermany	Adler & Bro. Fancy Goods, 439 7th Street west (1860)
ermany	Ordnance Bureau (1862)
ermany	
avaria [Germany]	240 Pennsylvania Avenue (1862)
ermany	
ermany	478 I Street south (1860)
ermany	478 I Street south (1860)
	407 11th Street west (1860)
anover [Germany]	499 7th Street west (1860)
odenberg [Germany]	
odenberg [Germany]	Behrend Brothers, 443 7th Street west (1860)
odenberg [Germany]	Gotthelf and Behrend Fancy Goods, 414 7th Street west (1860)
	420 7th Street west (1862)
odenberg [Germany]	
odenberg [Germany]	Behrend Brothers, 443 7th Street west (1860)
t. Croix	Home: 1 Madison Place (1860)
	374 D Street north (1865)
	M. Rosenbach & Company, 344 Pennsylvania Ave. (1862)
aryland	414 Pennsylvania Avenue (1862)
ermany	
ermany	Millinery, 401 7th Street west (1860)
oland	500 10th Street west (1862)
	Pennsylvania Avenue (1860)
	Home: 489 L Street north (1862)
oland	Boots and Shoes, 117 Pennsylvania Avenue (1860)
ermany	Home: H Street north, between 18th Street & 19th Street west (1862)
aryland	Home: H Street north, between 18th Street & 19th Street west (1862)
istrict of Columbia	Home: H Street north, between 18th Street & 19th Street west (1862)
istrict of Columbia	Home: H Street north, between 18th Street & 19th Street west (1862)
istrict of Columbia	Home: H Street north, between 18th Street & 19th Street west (1862)
russia [Germany]	224 G Street north (1862)
aden [Germany]	The Columbia, 7th Street & Louisiana Avenue (1865)
ustria	
ustria	
ermany	Clothing, 263 7th Street west (1860)
nited States	
nited States	
nited States	Clerk, Topographical Bureau (1860)

NAME	AGE (1860)	OCCUPATION
Fisher, Abraham	15	Clerk
Fisher, Morris	35	Shoemaker
Fishman, Hester	18	Milliner
Fishman, Solomon	42	Merchant
Freirich, Charles	24	Tobacconist
Gants, Samuel	44	Merchant
Gasdorf, Bernard		
Gassenheimer, Leopold	29	Merchant
Glick, Jonas		Clothier
Goldsmith, Simon	32	Merchant
Goldstein, Samuel/Selig	46	Pawnbroker
Goldstein, Rebecca	45	
Goldstein, Sarah	6	
Goldstein, Levi	3	
Gotthelf, Nathan	29	Merchant
Gotthelf, Julia		
Grossmayer, Nathan		
Gutman, Manuel	32	Merchant
Hamlein/Hamlin, Joseph		Merchant
Hammerschlag, C.		Baker & Confectioner
Hammerschlag, Herman	32	Paper Box Maker
Hammerschlag, Nathan		Baker & Confectioner
Hammerschlag, Siegfred		Baker & Confectioner
Hart, Abraham	29	Attorney
Hart, Bertha Swope		
Hartogensis, Edward S.	22	Clothier
Hartogensis, Fanny	21	Housekeeper
Heller, Simon	29	Merchant
Herman, Abraham		
Herman, Jacob		Clothier
Herzberg, Isaac		Pawnbroker
Hochherz, William		Hotel Operator
Horwitz, Phineas J.	38	Surgeon, U.S. Navy
Joseph, Joseph	40	Merchant
Joseph, Barbara	49	Housekeeper
Joseph, Barbara	14	
Joseph, Simon	12	
Joseph, Solomon	10	
Joseph, Miner	7	
Kaufman, Aaron	26	Merchant
Kaufman, Benjamin		Clothier
Kaufman, Emanuel	25	Merchant
Kaufman, Isaac	60	Merchant
Kaufman, Jonas		Clothier
Kaufman, Wolf	19	Clerk
King, Henry	24	Merchant
King, Samuel	21	Merchant
Kohn, Alois		Boarding House Owner
Lansburgh, Solomon		*Hazzan* (Cantor)
Lansburgh, Gustav	21	Merchant
Lansburgh, Max	11	Merchant
Lesser, G.H.		
Levy, Harry		Moneylender
Levy, Lawrence	35	Teacher
Levy, Serf		

PLACE OF BIRTH	HOME/BUSINESS LOCATION
Maryland	
Germany	Boots and Shoes, 287 Pennsylvania Avenue (1860)
Maryland	
Germany	Dry Goods, 391 7th Street west (1860)
Baden [Germany]	7th Street & Maryland Avenue, SW (1860)
Germany	
	Fancy Goods, 561 H Street north (1865)
Germany	Hats, Caps, & Gents' Furnishing Store, 385 7th Street west (1862)
	422 & 276 Pennsylvania Avenue (1860)
Germany	355 7th Street west
Russia	493 Massachusetts Avenue (1865)
Russia	Home: 493 Massachusetts Avenue (1865)
New York	Home: 493 Massachusetts Avenue (1865)
New York	Home: 493 Massachusetts Avenue (1865)
Hanover [Germany]	Gotthelf & Behrend Fancy Goods, 414 7th Street west (1860)
Hanover [Germany]	Home: 414 7th Street west (1860)
Merchant	274 Pennsylvania Avenue (1862)
Germany	
	Home: 554 New Jersey Avenue (1860)
	432 7th Street west & 409 Center Market (1862)
Hanover [Germany]	404 7th Street west (1860)
	432 7th Street west & 409 Center Market (1862)
	432 7th Street west & 409 Center Market (1862)
Osthoven [Germany]	Wolf & Hart, 344 Pennsylvania Avenue at 7th Street west (1865)
	Home: 565 12th Street west (1865)
Netherlands	683 7th Street west (1865)
Baden [Germany]	Home: 683 7th Street west (1865)
Germany	Millinery, 34 Market Space (1860)
	415 7th Street west (1865)
	429 Pennsylvania Avenue (1860)
	Clinton Hotel, 429 Pennsylvania Avenue (1862)
Maryland	Home: 444 12th Street west (1860)
Baden [Germany]	Boots and Shoes, 619 8th Street east (1860)
Bavaria [Germany]	Home: 556 9th Street east (1860)
Baden [Germany]	Home: 556 9th Street east (1860)
Baden [Germany]	Home: 556 9th Street east (1860)
Baden [Germany]	Home: 556 9th Street east (1860)
Baden [Germany]	Home: 556 9th Street east (1860)
Germany	Aaron & J Boots and Shoes, 510 7th Street west (1860)
	Home: 394 D Street north (1860)
Germany	
Germany	Dry Goods, 219 H Street north
	410 & 478 Pennsylvania Avenue (1865)
Germany	
Germany	Millinery and Fancy Goods, 294 Pennsylvania Avenue (1860)
Germany	Millinery and Fancy Goods, 289 Pennsylvania Avenue (1860)
	251 Pennsylvania Avenue (1865)
Prussia [Germany]	369 4th Street West (1860)
Hamburg [Germany]	Lansburgh M & Bro. Fancy Goods Agency, 322 C Street north (1860)
	Lansburgh M & Bro. Fancy Goods Agency, 322 C Street north (1860)
	Home: 548 Pennsylvania Avenue. (1865)
	414 Pennsylvania Avenue (1862)
Pennsylvania	

NAME	AGE (1860)	OCCUPATION
Liebermann, Charles	48	Doctor
Loewenthal, Julius		Attorney
Lulley, Emmanuel		Clothier
Lulley, Cecelia		
Lyon, Jacob	29	Treasury Dept. Laborer
Lyons, Ellis		Clothier
May, Myer		Boarding House Owner
Meyenberg, Solomon	32	Merchant
Meyenberg, Wolf		Merchant
Moses, Henry		
Mundheim, Simon	59	Shochet (ritual butcher)
Mundheim, Hannah	55	Housekeeper
Mundheim, Theresa	25	
Mundheim, Sara		
Nathan, Joseph		Merchant
Nordlinger, Bernard	29	Merchant
Nordlinger, Wolf		Merchant
Oppenheimer, Leopold	33	Merchant
Oppenheimer, Emma	32	Housekeeper
Oppenheimer, Sam	9	
Oppenheimer, Henry	7	
Oppenheimer, Sampson	5	
Oppenheimer, Isaac	3	
Oppenheimer, Caroline	2	
Oppenheimer, Manassas	40	Secondhand Clothier
Oppenheimer, Morris	7	Merchant
Oppenheimer, Hannah	33	
Oppenheimer, Simon	4	
Oppenheimer, Gustav	2	
Peyser, Jacob	29	Clothier
Peyser, Henriette	28	Domestic
Peyser, Henry	4	
Peyser, Eli	2	
Phillips, Philip	53	Lawyer
Phillips, Eugenia Levy	41	
Pinkus, Michael	35	Laborer
Poppers, Leon		Merchant
Rice, Abraham	45	Merchant
Rice, Louis	18	Clerk
Rosenthal, Emanuel	29	Merchant
Rosenthal, Emil	33	Merchant
Rothschild, William		Restauranteur
Samstag, M.	29	Merchant
Samstag, Samuel		Milliner
Sanger, Raphael	25	Clothier
Schlosberg, Bernard	18	Peddler
Schloss, Jacob	20	Merchant
Schwartz, Joseph	44	Clerk
Seldner, Lewis		Clothier
Seldner, Eva		Clothier
Sickle, Max	29	Merchant
Sickle, Rose	20	Milliner
Sickle, Sophie	23	Milliner

LACE OF BIRTH	HOME/BUSINESS LOCATION
ussia	
	207 Pennsylvania Avenue opposite Williard's (1865)
Iungary	389 7th Street west (1860)
	Home: 389 7th Street west (1860)
remen [Germany]	12 Ohio Avenue (1867)
	540 Pennsylvania Avenue (1865)
	Boots & Shoes, 344 7th Street west (1865)
Ianover [Germany]	Furs, 48 Market Space (1862)
Ianover [Germany]	Furs, 48 Market Space (1862)
Ianover [Germany]	Home: 349 Pennsylvania Avenue (1865)
Ianover [Germany]	Home: 349 Pennsylvania Avenue (1865)
Ianover [Germany]	Home: 349 Pennsylvania Avenue (1865)
Ianover [Germany]	Home: 349 Pennsylvania Avenue (1865)
	Nathan & Windholz, Columbia Garden, 559 12th Street (1865)
rance	Nordlinger & Brother, 114 Bridge Street, Georgetown (1866)
rance	Nordlinger & Brother, 114 Bridge Street, Georgetown (1866)
iermany	Clothing, 300 Pennsylvania Avenue (1860)
aden [Germany]	Home: 300 Pennsylvania Avenue (1860)
)istrict of Columbia	Home: 300 Pennsylvania Avenue (1860)
)istrict of Columbia	Home: 300 Pennsylvania Avenue (1860)
)istrict of Columbia	Home: 300 Pennsylvania Avenue (1860)
)istrict of Columbia	Home: 300 Pennsylvania Avenue (1860)
)istrict of Columbia	Home: 300 Pennsylvania Avenue (1860)
avaria [Germany]	
iermany	Clothing, 74 Louisiana Avenue (1860)
aden [Germany]	
)istrict of Columbia	
)istrict of Columbia	
russia [Germany]	485 9th Street west (1865)
aden [Germany]	
'irginia	
'irginia	
outh Carolina	462 16th Street west (1860)
outh Carolina	462 16th Street west (1860)
iermany	
Vetherlands	15 13½ Street west (1866)
iermany	Home: 498 10th Street west (1860)
iermany	Boots and Shoes, 8th Street east & I Street south (1860)
iermany	
iermany	Shoes, Pennsylvania Avenue (1860)
	295 Pennsylvania Avenue (1862)
iermany	Samstag and Hess Ales, Wines, &c., 10th Street west & Pennsylvania Avenue (1865)
	512 7th Street west (1860)
avaria [Germany]	297 7th Street west (1865)
ithuania	
Maryland	
iermany	Home: 222 22nd Street west (1860)
	Lewis Seldner & Co., 296, 346, 400 Pennsylvania Avenue (1862)
	Lewis Seldner & Co., 296, 346, 400 Pennsylvania Avenue (1862)
iermany	Millinery and Fancy Goods, Pennsylvania Avenue & 8th Street west (1860)
iermany	
iermany	

NAME	AGE (1860)	OCCUPATION
Siegel, Moses		Milliner
Silverberg, Bernard		Merchant
Solomon, Benjamin	28	Cigar Manufacturer
Solomons, Adolphus	34	Books/Stationery
Solomons, Rachel Seixas Phillips		
Strasburger, Henry	20	Pawnbroker
Strasburger, Jacob C.	26	Watch Repairman
Strasburger, Zody	17	Pawnbroker
Straus, Abraham	27	Merchant
Straus, Leopold	18	Clerk
Strauss, S.J.		
Strauss, Solomon		Clothier
Waldheimer, Marcus J.		
Weil, Rev. S.	23	*Hazzan* (Cantor)
Weinberger, Levi	16	Clerk
Weyl, Max	23	Watchmaker
Weyl, Miriam Raff		
Wolf, William		Clerk
Wolf, Simon	24	Lawyer
Wolfsheimer, Sam	23	Merchant
Yulee, David Levy	50	Senator
Zacharie, Isachar	33	Doctor

SOURCES: Robert Shosteck, "The Jewish Community of Washington, D.C., During the Civil War;" American Jewish Historical Quarterly, *Vol. 56, No.3 (March 1967) 319-347; Washington city directories,*

THE JEWISH COMMUNITY IN ALEXANDRIA, VIRGINIA, DURING THE CIVIL W

Note: Alexandria has changed its street-numbering system, so the addresses listed are not the same as today's addresses.

NAME	AGE (1860)	OCCUPATION
Alter, Samuel		Retail dealer
Baar, Lewis	29	Agent for mail service
Bendheim, David	33	Dry goods merchant
Bendheim, Leopold	30	Dry goods merchant
Bendheim, Caroline		
Bendheim, Moses	3	
Bendheim, Sophia	1	
Bernheimer, Samuel	15	Junk dealer
Blondheim, Henry	27	Clothier
Blondheim, Selic	64	
Blondheim, Simon	26	Clothier
Blondheim, Bertha		
Blondheim, Ester		
Brager, Joseph	31	Clothier
Brager, Isabella		
Brager, Ida		
Brown, Abraham	57	

LACE OF BIRTH	HOME/BUSINESS LOCATION
	Millinery & Fancygoods, 102 4 ½ Street west (1862)
	Fancy Dry Goods Store, 427 7th Street west (1865)
ngland	368 F Street north (1860)
ew York	Philp & Solomons, 332 Pennsylvania Avenue (1860)
ermany	
ermany	
ermany	Clothing, 320 D Street north (1860)
ermany	
	219 & 567 7th Street west (1865)
	MJ Waldheimer & Company,
	15th Street west & Pennsylvania Avenue (1865)
ermany	Home: 498 10th Street West
aryland	Clothing, 237 7th Street west (1865)
ürttemberg (Germany)	3rd Street & Pennsylvania Avenue (1861)
	520 Pennsylvania Avenue (1865)
	Wolf & Hart, 344 Pennsylvania Avenue at 7th Street west (1865)
ermany	Clothing, 614 8th Street east, and Millinery, 605 8th Street east (1860)
t. Thomas	262 I Street north (1860)
ngland	

LACE OF BIRTH	HOME/BUSINESS LOCATION
	Payne & Commerce Streets (1864)
esse-Cassel (Germany)	138 King Street (1860)
aden (Germany)	140 & 200 King Street (1867)
aden (Germany)	186 King Street (1867)
	Home: 285 King Street (1870)
aryland	Home: 285 King Street (1870)
aryland	Home: 285 King Street (1870)
ürttemberg (Germany)	Commerce & Payne Streets (1870)
esse-Darmstadt (Germany)	51 King Street (1860)
esse-Darmstadt (Germany)	Home: 93 Wolfe Street (1870)
esse-Darmstadt (Germany)	51 King Street (1867)
aryland	Home: King Street & Fairfax Street (1870)
	Home: King Street & Fairfax Street (1870)
russia (Germany)	12 & 55 King Street (1860)
aryland	Home: 72 Prince Street (1870)
	Home: 72 Prince Street (1870)
avaria (Germany)	

NAME	AGE (1860)	OCCUPATION
Dreifus, Julius	18	Junk dealer
Dreifus, Jenette		
Dreifus, Simpson	58	Rag merchant
Dreifus, Caroline		Junk dealer
Dreifus, Abraham		
Dreifus, Bettie		
Dreifus, Joseph		
Eichberg, Isaac	30	Dry goods merchant
Eichberg, Babette		
Einstein, Sam		Clerk
Einstein, Jane		
Feldenheimer, Joseph	25	
Genzberger, Leopold	39	Clothier
Genzberger, Bettie		
Kauffman, Joseph	22	Boot & shoe
Kauffman, Rosa		
Laupheimer, Michael	16	
Lindheimer, Samuel	26	Dry goods merchant
Meyenberg, Bettie		
Meyenberg, Solomon	32	Dry goods merchant
Meyenberg, Wolf		Dry goods merchant
Rosenthal, Emil	32	Spoke & sumac mills
Rosenthal, Ernestine		
Rosenthal, Julius		
Rosenthal, Sallie		
Rosenthal, Martha		
Rosenthal, Bertha		
Rosenthal, I.		Boot & shoe
Rosenthal, Myer		
Rosenthal, Joseph		
Rosenthal, Samuel		
Reuben, Moritz	27	Junk dealer
Reuben, Caroline		
Reuben, Leopold		
Reuben, Daniel		
Reuben, Sara		
Rich, Hannah	6	
Seldner, Peter		
Schwarz, Henry	27	Milliner
Schwarz, Jennie		
Schwarz, Isaac	25	Clothier
Schwarz, Lena		
Shoenthal, Joseph		
Stein, Lewis	26	Groceries
Stein, Cecelia		
Strauss, Henry	24	Boot & shoe
Ullman, Maurice		
Vogelheim, Joseph		
Waterman, Simon	51	Clothier/merchant
Waterman, Bettie		
Weinberg, Emma	14	

SOURCES: Addresses from Alexandria city directories published 1860, 1867 and 1870

PLACE OF BIRTH	HOME/BUSINESS LOCATION
Württemberg (Germany)	8 Union Street (1870)
Württemberg (Germany)	Home: Payne Street near Duke Street (1870)
	11 Commerce Street (1867)
Württemberg (Germany)	66 Duke Street (1870)
Württemberg (Germany)	8 Union Street (1870)
Württemberg (Germany)	Home: Payne Street near Duke Street (1870)
Hengstfeld, Württemberg (Germany)	
Bavaria (Germany)	22 N Royal Street (1860)
Baden (Germany)	190 King Street (1867)
New York	Home: 29 North Fairfax Street (1870)
Germany	
Baden (Germany)	103 King Street/101 King Street (1867)
Hanover (Germany)	
Hanover (Germany)	King Street & Pitt Street (1860)
Hanover (Germany)	King Street & Pitt Street (1860)
Lichtenau, Baden (Germany)	Duke Street & Strand Street (1870)
	Home: 65 South Fairfax Street (1870)
District of Columbia	Home: 65 South Fairfax Street (1870)
District of Columbia	Home: 65 South Fairfax Street (1870)
District of Columbia	Home: 65 South Fairfax Street (1870)
District of Columbia	Home: 65 South Fairfax Street (1870)
	98 King Street (1860)
	98 King Street (1867)
Poland	
Ohio	
Ohio	
Ohio	
Bavaria (Germany)	96 King Street (1870)
Bavaria (Germany)	132 King Street (1860)
Bavaria (Germany)	7 King Street (1860)
	Home: 15 South Royal Street (1870)
Barmstedt (Germany)	20 N Royal (1870)
Ohio	
Bavaria (Germany)	148 King Street (1867)
Germany	100 King Street (1860)
Hesse (Germany)	

INDEX

A

Abraham, Abraham 67
Abram, Ellis 77-78
Adams, Charles Francis 75
Adas Israel Congregation
(Washington, DC) 34, 53, 99, 110
Adler, Adolph 117
Adler, Morris 121
Adler, Samuel 68
Alexandria Gazette 30, 44
Alexandria, VA 8, 9, 22, 23, 28, 30, 31
Allen, Michael 63
Alschuler, Samuel 60
Angle, Myer 71
Anshe Maariv, Congregation
(Chicago, IL) 60
Antisemitism 16-18, 46, 47, 58, 75-79, 100, 103
Arnold, Isaac 73, 74

B

B'nai B'rith 20, 27, 33, 34, 50, 51, 52, 109, 124, 149
B'nai Israel Congregation
(New York, NY) 57
Baar, Levi 137
Baker, Lafayette C. 51
Bar, Levy 120
Barr, Louis 131
Barton, Clara 53
Baum, Henry 31
Baum, Leonard 139
Beecher, Henry Ward 122
Beggardt, Isaac 124, 139
Behrend, Adajah 39, 121, 138
Behrend, Bendiza 137
Behrend, Bernhard 8, 39
Behrend, Michael 121
Benjamin, Judah P. 12, 46, 49, 58, 76, 77
Benjamin, Park 122
Biggardt, J. 137
Burgauer, G. 124
Beth Ahabah (Richmond, VA) 71

Beth El Hebrew Congregation
(Alexandria, VA) 9, 30, 37, 44, 46
Beth Israel (Macon, GA) 45
Binswanger, Augustus 121, 122
Board of Delegates of American Israelites 15, 54, 109
Bondi, August 86
Booth, John Wilkes 9, 35, 36
Brady, Mathew 27, 99
Brown, John 77
Bruckheimer, Moses 145
Bull Run, First Battle of 8
Bull Run, Second Battle of 8, 40, 44, 45, 145
Butler, Benjamin 43, 88, 89, 90

C

Camp Parole, MD 45
Chase, Salmon P. 101
Clay, Henry 61
Cochel, C.T. 118
Cohen, Eleanor H. 88
Cohen, G. 136
Cohen, J.H. 121
Cohen, Levi 121
Cohen, Mark 121
Cohen, Matilda 93
Cohnheim, Max 28, 122, 125, 135-137, 146
Collis, Septima Levy 92, 94, 95
Collis, Charles H. T. 92
Columbia 28, 135-138, 146
Cox, Oliver 118

D

del Banco, Max 13
Davis, Jefferson 43, 46, 47, 77, 81
DeCordova, Raphael J. 122, 136
Deleeuw, M.R. 57
Dreifus, Bettie 31
Dreifus, Caroline 30
Dreifus, Simpson 30
Du Bois, John Van Deusen 104

E

Ellinger, Lewis 124
Emanu-El, Temple (New York, NY) 68, 92
Evening Star 115
Ezekiel, Catherine Francis Hamlin 86
Ezekiel, Jacob 73
Ezekiel, Moses 19, 20, 72, 86

F

Ferry, Thomas W. 99
Fischel, Arnold 15, 54, 64
Foote, Henry S. 76
Forney, John W. 122
Ford's Theatre 9, 35
Fort Stevens 9, 25
Frank, Rosa 40
Frankel, Jacob 64
Free Sons of Israel 120
Freedman, Max 63, 64
Friedlander, Max 25
Fuchs, Henrietta 145

G

Gardner, Alexander 53, 55, 57, 133
Garfield, James 52
General Orders Number 11 8, 9, 16-18, 32-34, 64-66, 100-110, 136
Georgetown University 36, 39
Gerst, Mary 74
Gettysburg, Battle of 9, 38, 58
Gintzberger, Henry 71, 72
Gotthelf, Nathan 137
Gotthold, Isaac 122, 136
Grand Army of the Republic 40
Grant, Jesse 17, 65, 104
Grant, Ulysses S. 8, 9, 16-18, 32-34, 52, 53, 64-66, 99-110
Grant, Ulysses, Jr. 99
Gratz, Rebecca 96
Greeley, Horace 122
Greenhow, Rose O'Neal 42, 43
Grossmayer, Nathan 143-144
Gurley, John A. 17
Gusdorf, Bernard 121, 124
Gutman, A.A. 121
Gutman, Emanuel 117

H

Halleck, Henry 18, 33, 106
Hammerschlag, C. 130
Hammerslough, Julius 59
Hanlein, Joseph 117
Harmonie Club 27, 122, 124
Harold, David 36
Hart, Abraham 40, 139
Hart, Alexander 74-75
Hay, John 50, 52
Heilbroun, H. 37
Herman, Abraham 121
Herman, Jacob 121
Herman, Samuel 116
Herzberg, Isaac 117, 121
Hildensheim, J. 139
Hill, S.P. 118
Hirsch, Isaac 72
Hochheimer, Henry 118, 126
Hochherz, William 139
Hoffheimer, Sol 124
Horwitz, Jonathan (Phineas J.) 138
Hyneman, Jacob E. 73

I

Isaacs, Meyer 62, 68

J

Jewish Messenger, The 13, 22, 23, 24, 26, 28, 54, 62, 119
Johnson, Andrew 75, 76, 144
Jonas, Abraham 59

K

Karpeles, Leopold 9, 38, 142
Kasche, Ferdinand 135
Kaskel, Cesar 17, 18, 33, 66, 106
Kaufman, A. 131
Kaufman, Benjamin 121, 146
Kaufman, Jonas 121
Kaufmann, Samuel 131
Kelton, John C. 106, 107
Koch, Werner 135, 137, 138
Kohn, Abraham 60

Kohn, Alois 139
Korn, Bertram W. 149
Kronheimer, L. 138
Kuttner, Henry 33

L

Lansburgh and Bro. Department Store 28, 137
Lansburgh, Gustav 9, 28, 37, 148
Lansburgh, Max 9, 28, 37, 148
Lansburgh, S. 115
Lazarus, Rachel Mordecai 88
Lee, Robert E. 13, 18, 20, 35, 73, 74, 81
Leeser, Isaac 11, 14, 19, 37, 115, 118, 119, 120, 122, 123, 124
Lesser, G.H. 122
Leterman, Hannah 73
Leterman, Isaac 73
Leterman, Simon 73
Levy, Abraham I. 73
Levy, C.M. 11
Levy, David Cardoza 94
Levy, E. J. 73
Levy, Harry 121
Levy, Henry 130
Levy, Isaac J. 73
Levy, Jacob A. 73
Levy, Jonas M. 41, 141
Levy, Jonas Phillips 41, 114, 115, 116, 120
Levy, Rosena 74
Levy, Serf 121
Levy, Uriah Phillips 41
Liebermann, Charles 25, 36
Lilienthal, Max 18
Lissberger, Herman 114
Literary and Dramatic Association 20, 122, 123, 125, 136, 149
Loewenthal, Julius 137, 139
Louis, Rachel Semon 82
Lyons, Ellis 122

M

Mannheimer, Israel 25
Manheimer, Joseph H. 122
May, Myer 139
Mayer, Carrie 87
Mayer, Emma 87
Mayer, Ophelia 87
McClellan, George B. 133
Melle, H. 115
Michelbacher, Maximilian 73, 74, 78
Mikveh Israel (Philadelphia) 37
Miller, Nehemiah H. 138
Monticello 41
Mordecai, Emma 81, 88, 96
Mordecai, Alfred 48
Moses, Henry 121
Mount Pleasant Hospital 38
Mount Sinai Society 45
Mundheim, Hannah 38, 142
Mundheim, Sara 38, 142
Mundheim, Simon 27, 142

N

Nathan, Joseph 137
Newman, John P. 99
Nordlinger, Bernard 45, 145

O

Oak Hill Cemetery 47
Occident, The 39, 114, 116, 117, 118, 119, 139
Oppenheimer, Leopold 121
Order Number 11
(see General Orders Number 11)

P

Peixotto, Benjamin F. 34, 109, 110
Pember, Phoebe Yates Levy 87, 90-91, 92
Phillips, Eugenia Levy 8, 42, 43, 86, 89, 90
Phillips, Phillip 42-43
Philp and Solomons 37, 53, 54, 55, 57, 132, 133, 134, 135, 137, 148
Philp, Franklin 53, 132
Poore, Ben. Perley 133
Pribram, Solomon 114

R

Raphall, Morris 11, 59
Rice, Henry 60
Rich, Herbert 40
Richmond Enquirer 77
Richmond Examiner 78-79
Rider, Solomon A. 122
Rosenthal, Albert 80
Rosenthal, Joseph 31, 80
Rothschild, William 139
Ryan, W.M.D. 118

S

Salomon, Edward 107
Sanitary Commission, United States 26, 64, 92-93, 142
Sax, Jacob 25
Schlessinger, L. 30
Schwarz, Henry 44, 79
Schwarz, Isaac 44
Seldner, L. 137
Seldner, Peter 81
Semons Family 82
Shearith Israel, Congregation
(New York, NY) 67, 92
Sherman, William T. 100, 103
Ship Island 43, 90
Siegel, G. 124
Siegel, Moses 117
Silverberg, Bernard 131
Simson, I 124
Slavery 8, 9, 25, 58
Sneersohn, H.Z. 109
Solomon, Clara 87-88
Solomon, Solomon 87
Solomon, S.N. 121
Solomons, Adolphus 53, 54, 55, 132, 133
Spiegel, Caroline Frances Hamlin 79, 85, 92, 94, 95, 96
Spiegel, Marcus 12, 79, 85, 94, 95, 103
Stanton, Edwin 51
Stein (Stern), Charles 145
Stevens, Atherton H. 81

Strasberg, Henry 121
Strauss, S.J. 121
Strauss, Solomon 121
Strouse, Myer 124
Surratt, Mary 35
Surratt, John 36

T

Tasitro, L.F. 125
Teller, Raphael 124
Trounstine, Philip 65, 105

V

Valandigham, Clement L. 63
Vasen, G. 124

W

Waldheimer, Marcus J. 122
Wallach, Richard 118
Washburne, Elihu 65
Washington Arsenal (Fort McNair) 48
Washington Hebrew Congregation 9, 19, 20, 26, 27, 36, 37, 38, 39, 40, 41, 45, 46 50, 52, 99, 113, 114-120, 125-126, 142, 146
Waterman, Simon 31, 80
Waterman, Caroline 80
Weil, M.H. 124
Weil, Samuel 26, 116, 119, 126
Weygand, Nicholas 135
Weyl, Max 121, 131
Whitlock, Philip 77, 78
Whitman, Walt 140
Wise, Isaac Mayer 11, 18, 26, 30, 66, 67, 122, 136
Wolcott, Christopher P. 105, 107
Wolf, Simon 20, 35, 50-52, 96, 110, 119, 121, 122, 124, 125, 132, 138, 139, 140, 141, 142
Wolf, William 121

Y

Yulee, David Levy 47, 75, 76

Z

Zacharie, Isachar 49, 60-63